Science, Technology,

And The Texture of Our Lives

Thomas Oberdan

Third Edition

Published by Tavenner Publishing Co., Anderson, South Carolina

ISBN 978-1-937435-65-3

For Angelina, who never winced...

Acknowledgements

The contributions of my colleagues in the Science and Technology in Society Program at Clemson University has proved invaluable in both the conception and execution of this project. Since the program's inception, Pam Mack, has been a constant source of encouragement and friendship. Cecil Huey's contribution to the views presented here, coming from a perspective alien to my own viewpoint, has been enlightening indeed. Most of all, Cecil's friendship, care, and continuous stimulation at times when that was nearly impossible, went far beyond the call of friendship. Indispensable in the final stages of the project have been the contributions of Scott Brame, Elizabeth Stansell Anderson and Angelina Oberdan. To all these, as well as the multitude of Clemson students who have passed through my classes, offering questions and challenges which have illuminated my grasp of these issues, I extend my heartfelt thanks.

TABLE OF CONTENTS

1 INTRODUCTION   8
Science and Technology in Daily Life   10
Causes and Effects   14
Determinism   17
A Critical Approach   19
Problems   21
Prospects   23

2 SCIENCE AND TECHNOLOGY: 30
The Aims of Science and Technology   32
Critical Questions   37
The Pessimistic Meta-Induction   38
"Theories," "Hypotheses," and "Laws"   44
Historical Trends in the Relations of Science and
Technology   50
Technological Stimulation of Science   54

3 METHODS   62
Belief   64
Justification of Beliefs   66
Types of Arguments   68
Deductive Validity   72
Conditionals   74
Logical Independence   77
Statistical Arguments   80

4 TESTING   92
Explanation and Prediction   94
The Hypothetico-Deductive Model   98
Falsification   103
Crucial Experiments   105
The Shape of the Earth   109
Observational Evidence   110

5 DYNAMICS   **118**
Incremental Improvement   *119*
Long-Term Development   *122*
Scientific Revolutions   *125*
Copernicus' Innovation   *130*
Revolutions in Technology   *134*

6 THE SOCIAL CONTEXT   **142**
Social Groups   *142*
Social Consequences   *145*
Luddism   *148*
Technological Fixes   *149*
Technological Determinism   *154*
Social Constructionism   *159*
Conclusion   *159*

1
INTRODUCTION

We shall find in the experience
of the past, in the observation of
the progress that the sciences and
civilization have already made,
in the analysis of the progress
of the human mind and of the
development of its faculties, the
strongest reasons for believing
that nature has set no limit to
the realization of our hopes.

Marquis de Condorcet,
*Sketch for a Historical Picture of
the Progress of the Human Mind*

The topics of science and technology make up much of the
fare of daily discussions, in forms ranging from congressional
debates to news reports, to casual exchanges in social settings.
With the press of a button or the twist of a dial, one can hear a story
about the most recent space launch, or the next one. Or perhaps
our elected representatives are disputing the merits of funding
a round of medical research that promises a breakthrough that
may save millions of lives. Or one might be told a story about the
development of a new gizmo, which will provide the user with
audio or video entertainment. And while there is no denying
the importance of scientific and technological developments
among the concerns of newscasters, congressmen, and "those

in the know," these concerns merely draw attention to deeper issues about science and technology.

Far more significant than the high profile of science and technology among current events is the matter of how the course of daily life—the minute-by-minute, nitty-gritty—wends its way, under, around, and through a jungle of scientific results and technological innovations. Indeed, there is <u>no single aspect of our lives</u>, no matter how private or intimate, <u>which has not been invaded</u>, occupied, and annexed by science and technology.

Mill Workers Changing Bobbins

The hiker lost in the wilderness, leaving the trappings of civilization far behind, still relies on his global positioning device to learn his location. The vigil candles in churches have given way to electric devices which light up (for a timed interval) when the penitent inserts a coin in the slot! Even the Amish, who generally eschew the science and technology of recent centuries for that of earlier ones, feel safer with a telephone (especially a cellphone!) available nearby (though not in their homes!) in case of medical emergencies. It is simply impossible to exaggerate the extent to which science and technology have reached into the daily lives of everyone on the planet, touching the ways they work and play, interact and mingle.

Science and Technology in Daily Life

Science and technology are so intimately bound up with the path traced by our lives that it is simply no longer possible to conceive of either as separable and independent from the stuff of human existence. Science and technology are as much a part of our lives as the most human of our activities, the most intimate of our exchanges with each other, as are those distinctively human thoughts and feelings that make us the creatures we are. In short, science and technology can no longer be set up as objects of study, for the purposes of analysis and inquiry, apart from the lives they permeate. The net result is that the flavor of the day-to-day course of our lives—its very texture—has been shaped and formed by science and technology. Hence the concern of this book.

But to raise this concern is, at the same time, to provoke another, related matter. And that is just the question of what control, if any, can be exerted over the role of science and technology in daily life. The most obvious (and least satisfying) answer to this question is to refer to the fact that, in a democratic society, citizens are called upon to judge the future course of scientific investigation and technological development by voting for or against political candidates who favor a particular policy for

Hikers with GPS

people control the role of S&T when voting for office

science and technology. Typically, they promise—if elected, of course—to dump billions of taxpayer dollars into its future. Or, in what is perhaps a more familiar scenario, political nominees think a particular line of scientific inquiry should be stifled, because it conflicts with their religious tenets. On the other hand, they might think it should be encouraged, because the best experts tell them it holds great promise to solve certain pressing social problems. In either case, voters are being asked to choose the direction in which science and technology, funded by their own dollars, will advance.

Superconducting Super Collider

Projected Superconducting Super Collider

An enlightening example can be drawn from a brief history of the Superconducting Super Collider (SSC), a particle accelerator slated in the 1980's to be constructed in Texas. The SSC was proposed as a technological aid to investigate some of the most fundamental questions in particle physics, the science that explores the properties of sub-atomic particles by colliding them at extraordinarily high energies. In fact, the SSC was planned to produce collisions at three times the energy levels of the Large Hadron Collider, operated by the European Organization for Nuclear Research (CERN) in Geneva. At least part of the motivation for building the SSC was that American physicists feared they were losing their lead in elementary particle physics to the Europeans, who were spending twice as much on elementary particle research. The SSC would aid in the restoration of the American priority in particle physics by answering key questions about the Standard Model, which posited two types of sub-atomic physics –quarks and leptons- governed by three forces. These questions impeded any further advance in the field and could be answered by the production of a Higgs boson, which only an accelerator with the power of the SSC could produce.[1]

The SSC was first designed in a study conducted in 1983. As the design was finalized and the first stages of construction began, the SSC became the focus of a heated debate over costs. In 1987, Congress was informed that the project would cost no more than $4.4 billion. Congress voted in 1989 to spend $225 million in 1990 on the project, committing itself to funding the project at a cost of $5.9 billion But by 1993, cost projections had risen to more than $13 billion. Roughly the same amount was simultaneously requested for NASA's involvement in the International Space Station, and the argument was raised that budgetary constraints prevented funding both projects. Strong lobbying efforts were launched promoting the SSC project; the President of the United States even invited hesitant legislators to the White House to meet persuasive physicists who supported the collider. These efforts were largely motivated by the economic boom the SSC would bring to the area of Texas, south of the Trinity River. But they were undermined by the release of reports, by governmental and independent agencies, criticizing the high costs of the SSC and the incompetence of its management. Finally, in October of 1993, the project was cancelled by Congress. Although there are a number of reasons for terminating the SSC, the political efforts by elected representatives and their final votes were largely based on their wish to pursue the economic interests of their constituents. The salient point is that, in a somewhat indirect way, individual citizens can determine the course of technological development and scientific research.[3]

In this way, science and technology are shaped and influenced by society just as much as dramatic developments in science or technology—like a cure for a particularly virulent disease—influence society. Thus, society acts as a causal force shaping and molding the science and technology of the future, every bit as much as science and technology exert a causal influence on society. And that is why understanding science and technology requires, first and foremost, the realization that neither science nor technology can be fully comprehended apart from the societies in which they are conceived, develop, and flourish or fail.

These concerns can be answered if there were some method of predicting the future reach of developments in science and technology and what can be done to control them. However, the only plausible means available is to compare current directions with past ones and to examine their effects on the society of the time and the measures that were undertaken to control and limit, or perhaps promote and encourage, particular developments. Thus, in this case as in so many others, understanding the future requires a feeling and appreciation of current trajectories stimulated by past developments. It is only from the past that one can glean some idea of what the future holds—because it is only from an understanding of how various factors have shaped recent and current events that some idea might emerge of how their combination will shape events in the future. History may or may not repeat itself, but certainly many of the same forces—or similar ones—that shaped past events will shape future ones. Of that, there can be no dispute.

The effort of this text will be directed towards the goal of developing a conceptual understanding of its subject, an understanding, which though independent of any factual matters, nonetheless reflects what has indeed been the case.

That is to say, even though the validity of the conclusions that are reached do not directly depend on a specified set of historical contingencies, their usefulness as a guide to the future will naturally depend on their applicability to contemporary situations. At the same time, the goal is to conceive science and technology with sufficient breadth to understand their delicate interplay with social conditions. This means not only an appreciation of the social consequences of scientific discoveries or technological innovations, but also a recognition of the social forces that shape and influence the direction of scientific investigation and technological innovation.

In short, the goal of this essay is to develop a broad conceptual understanding of science and technology, which reflects the integral role of social forces in their development. If it succeeds, the result will not be a collection of answers to a pre-determined set of outstanding questions, a sort of binary questionnaire evoking "thumbs up" and "thumbs down" responses. Rather, what is sought is a vantage point from which to observe and reflect on how thoroughly science and technology permeate the course of daily life.

The point, then, is nothing less than a critical perspective, neither disparagingly negative nor enthusiastically positive. The aim is a perspective that grasps, in the broadest possible conceptual terms, the meaning and significance of science and technology as it is embedded in day-to-day reality.

Causes and Effects

Even a simple grasp of causality will serve quite well as a starting-point. Of course, the kinds of things causality relates to are usually events, as in the classical example of two billiard balls colliding. Imagine an eight-ball, resting peacefully on a pool table. Then a cue ball careens across the green felt headed directly for the eight. First, the cue ball collides into the eight and then the

Contingent coincidences — the two things aren't related at all.

eight travels on its way. In this there are two events: the collision of the balls and the motion of the eight-ball; the collision is the cause and the subsequent motion of the eight-ball is the effect.

In other cases, it is more illuminating to conceive causes and effects as conditions, particularly the conditions of material objects. Take any object exposed to sunlight, focusing on its exposure as the condition operating as a cause. After a sufficient period of time, the object warms, the effect of exposure to the sun. Analyzed this way, it appears that causality relates the conditions described as exposure to the sun (on the one hand) and increasing temperature (on the other hand).

Of course, there are countless cases in which two events, or a couple of different kinds of conditions, are regularly associated. Among these associations, only some are recognized as ones involving a causal connection. Those that do not involve causality are just contingent coincidences, relations between events or conditions which might just as well not be associated at all. For instance, there is no causality linking the color of John's shirt and the date of his friend's birthday. It is, rather, just a coincidence that John is wearing a green shirt and his friend was born on April 19th. The contingency of this association is readily evident from the fact that John's friend might just as well have been born on April 20th and that it would not affect the color of his shirt one bit.

What is missing in the cases where the association between two events or conditions is merely accidental is some sense of necessity--that is, the idea that if the antecedent event or condition (i.e., the cause) occurred, then the effect just had to follow. In other words, any billiard ball at rest that is struck by a moving ball must move. Or, any substantial object exposed to direct sunlight must grow warmer.

And these "musts" are what distinguish genuinely causal relations from accidental ones. And that is because scientists and engineers, when investigating some phenomenon, want to know "why" a given event or condition always follows another particular event or condition. They would certainly never accept "Stuff happens" for an answer! This does not imply that other causes might not have brought about the same effect. Indeed, there is often an event or condition other than the actual cause which might also have had the same effect, provided, of course, that this other event or condition had existed at the time. And, as many of the examples used in later explanations make apparent, the fact that there are possible alternative causes can aggravate the difficulty of analyzing a particular case.

One of the most effective ways to accentuate the difference between causal relations and purely accidental ones is by saying that the causal relations are expressed by natural laws. Natural laws are statements of the form

> All objects which possess the property F also possess the property G.

or, more briefly,

> All F are G.

Here one can easily imagine that F is the property of, for instance, being a country located near the equator and that G represents a warm climate. Then, the schematic sentence above might just say

> All countries located near the equator have warm climates.

A statement like this one is generally called "lawlike" to direct the focus on its form, rather than whether it's true or false. In such statements, like the one above, the properties F and G are said to be causally rather than accidentally linked. That is just what the lawfulness is all about! Then, of course, a natural

causal relation ⟹ lawlike statement

law is just a true lawlike statement. A rather straightforward understanding of causal connections is the one that relates them to lawlike statements.

But this raises further questions. How do individuals, with little or no technical training in science or technology, relate these lawlike statements, to their everyday lives? How can lay people bring the particular events of their everyday existence to bear on generalizations beginning with the phrase "For all..."? The question of the relation between highly technical universal statements, and the individual occurrences which make up daily life, are at the center of inquiries into science and technology in society.

The situation is simply this: on the one hand, there are the generalizations which form the laws of science, and, on the other, there are individual situations involving scientific, technological, and social factors operating as specific causes. Since it is these particular, individual causes, which affect the course of everyday life, it becomes absolutely essential to develop the capacity to relate generalized, lawlike statements to individual situations.

Determinism

Discussions of causality always lead to the question of determinism, the issue of whether the present is determined by the past and the future determined by the present.

In his *Philosophical Treatise of Probabilities*, Pierre-Simon La- Place envisioned a super-intellect, later referred to as "LaPlace's Demon," whose intelligence was so powerful that it could grasp the values of all the

Pierre-Simon LaPlace.

essential physical parameters of every particle in the universe in a given moment.[4]

From this knowledge about the disposition of the universe at the present time, the Demon could deduce the physical character of every object in the universe for any other time. Apart from the question whether the kind of cognitive power exemplified by the Demon will ever be realized—by some kind of super-computer, say—there is the separate and distinct question of the causal relations between physical configurations (or events) at earlier and later times. Then the question is whether the state of the universe at any given time is nothing but the effect of its state at some earlier instant. LaPlace answered this question without any ambiguity when he wrote:

> *We may regard the present state*
> *of the universe as the effect of its*
> *past and the cause of its future.*

As LaPlace understands it, determinism is just the idea that antecedent factors wholly fix later conditions.

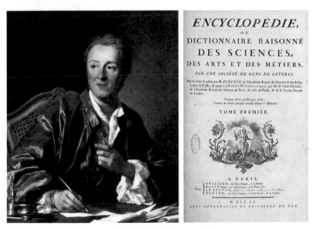

Denis Diderot

Of course, whether or not determinism is true of the physical universe is a matter to be decided by physicists. And this very question led to celebrated disputes in the early 20th Century between physicists as eminent as Niels Bohr and Albert Einstein. And certainly the issue of determinism is difficult to decide when all of the factors involved belong to the same basic kind, like physical events.

But the difficulty increases exponentially when it involves elements as diverse as scientific, technological, and social ones. And there is a perfectly valid question of whether the kinds of causal interactions which occur among scientific achievements, technological innovations, and social developments, are deterministic. Do scientific achievements determine which technologies are developed? Are technological artifacts merely the products of applying scientific results to particular situations? Is technology just applied science?

It is just as reasonable to wonder whether every technology has the same effects on every society to which it is introduced. Do technologies produce social consequences just as deterministically as the collision of a moving billiard ball and one at rest causes the motion of the latter? In short, do technological advances drive the course of society? Is social progress dependent on technological innovation? These questions are among the largest that have ever faced the study of science, technology, and society. All of them involve the analysis of the complex causal relations prevailing among the disparate kinds of elements involved. Yet the issues, which arise, are among the most pressing issues confronting any study of human affairs because of the dominant role of beliefs about these matters in the conventional wisdom

A Critical Approach

Obviously, contemporary thinking about science and technology in society involves many complex ideas that can hardly be grasped without serious training. This is even more evident when one realizes the difficulties and complexities of assessing the merits of such claims in the effort to determine whether they are true or false. Since that is exactly the aim of the present effort, it will be necessary to include intensive study of methods and tactics for the analysis of these ideas. To keep things simple, the overall effort of analysis of claims can be reduced to a basic strategy consisting of three straightforward steps.

Analysis: The first is analysis of the statement or the arguments advanced in it behalf. This amounts to answering the question, what must the world be like if this claim is true? The statement or the arguments advanced in its support will give you the answer to this question. First and foremost, this will require careful assessment of the inferential connections between supporting statements and the one in question. But it will also be necessary to uncover any assumptions which have been silently adopted. Once assumptions are discovered, the conditions of their truth must be delineated.

Evidence: The next step is the determination of the extent to which the world really is the way it would have to be for the statement in question (and its underlying assumptions) are true. This just raises the

Steam Engine

question of the evidence offered in behalf of the statement in question. This is largely an analytic task, since the burden of proof for producing evidence falls on the proponents of a claim. It is not up to others, who are presented with the case of the statement, to go digging for the truth.

Synthesis: Finally, it is time to put it all back together again. The idea here is that ideas from disparate sources -whether they are any of the original ideas or not hardly matters- are synthesized or brought together to provide different perspectives on the same topic as the original statement under scrutiny. This requires imagination but the creative process will improved with practice. Before you know it, you'll be thinking of alternative explanations of the matters up for dispute which are far more plausible than the statement with which you began. That's thinking!

Although you will undoubtedly learn much about the development of science and technology, especially in their myriad relations to society, there is much, much more to the study of science and technology. And that is the hope that, in the process of assimilating the ideas presented here, you will also increase your critical abilities and become a much more incisive thinker about the topics of this book. And a lot of other things!

Problems

The most widespread belief of the conventional wisdom is that technology drives progress. The concept of progress, of course, is the gift of the Enlightenment thinkers of the 18th Century--Voltaire, Diderot, and D'Alembert in France, Thomas Jefferson and Ben Franklin in the United States, Adam Smith in Scotland, and Immanuel Kant in Prussia, as well as countless others too numerous to mention. Inspired by the science of Isaac Newton and the political writings of John Locke, these thinkers envisioned a future for mankind consisting of continuous progress. And progress, as they understood it, included not only improvement of the material conditions of everyday life but in the prevailing social arrangements. In other words, while the standard of living would continuously increase so, too, would individual members of society become free and equal.

These ideas were imported to America in wholesale fashion by the envoys of the Enlightenment who became the Founding Fathers of the United States. One can readily see, for instance, the prevalence of these ideals in Jefferson's vision of republican democracy. But before Jefferson's vision could be realized, the Industrial Revolution arrived, and Americans began to focus exclusively on material progress, forgetting the broader concerns of their Enlightenment forefathers.

Although the Industrial Revolution produced remarkable achievements, from the steamship, to the railroads, to the telegraph, it also yielded a plethora of inexpensive goods, which acted as a palliative for the laboring masses. Progress, in any form other than the material, was postponed as the rich got richer and the poor got poorer until social unrest brought the efforts to correct social injustice, collectively known as "The Progressive Era." But the social and spiritual progress which the Enlightenment thinkers valued so highly were overwhelmed and forgotten by the remarkable advances in technology, and the material progress the new productivity yielded.

The end-result was that Americans came to identify progress in purely materialistic terms, blithely believing that progress in any other respect was a natural consequence of improvements in the material conditions of existence. Thus progress came to mean material progress, technology was seen as its driver, and science was regarded as the source of technological innovation. In short, science drives technology, which, in its turn, drives progress.

This understanding of how science, technology, and society interact dominates conventional thinking. Indeed, the prevailing paradigm can be summarized in three precepts:

> *Technological innovation rests on scientific findings.*
>
> *Technological advance produces social benefits.*
>
> *Social problems can be remedied by technological means.*

These tenets seem so obviously true that no one would dispute them. Indeed, they lie at the very foundations of what passes for received wisdom in the contemporary world. Nonetheless, when examined closely, they are all deceptively, misleadingly false. And it is the goal of this text to develop the analytic tools that anyone can use to reveal their failure.

Prospects

This effort begins in the next chapter, which focuses on the fundamental concepts of science and technology, as well as their most salient differences. Quickly the subject-matter reveals its own inner complexity and the daunting challenge faced by any attempt to reduce it to sound-bites, bumper stickers, or simplistic truisms.

Indeed, it soon becomes obvious that any effort to engage science and technology must, as a beginning, address questions about how concepts are formed and ideas adopted. But this task requires a grasp of the rudiments of deductive and statistical reasoning, the subject-matter of Chapter 3. These tools are then applied to the testing and adoption of theoretical beliefs— conceived broadly to include not just scientific ideas but the images of reality presupposed by technical efforts to solve problems. The discussion begins by focusing on the derivation of predictions from theoretical hypotheses. Once derived, predictions are then confronted with evidence in the form of regimented observations or controlled experiments.

The ins and outs of deriving predictions comprise the first topic addressed in Chapter 4. But the discussion also treats the difficult question of how predictions are related to the evidence of observation and experiment. Of course, the ultimate value of predictions lies in the implications of their empirical evaluation for the hypotheses, which originally spawned them, a matter that forms the final topic of the chapter.

The next chapter turns to a consideration of how science and technology develop over time. The discussion focuses particularly on how the incremental, cumulative development of technology contrasts with the bi-modal development of science. Like technology, science passes through periods exhibiting a developmental dynamic, which is both incremental and cumulative. But, in science, these stages are punctuated by radical change. And it is these punctuations, or revolutions, which give us pause. The chapter closes with reflections on some of the implications these differences in dynamics bear for any understanding of the relationship between science and technology. In Chapter 6, the conceptual tools developed in the previous chapters are employed to consider how science and technology are situated in society, which leads to a discussion of the implications of the distinctively social character of science and technology. In closing, some suggestions are offered for using the tools and models developed for further reflections on the saturation of daily life by science and technology.

It is not to be expected that the value of these investigations and reflections lies in the support they provide for broad, sweeping conclusions about the integration of science and technology in daily life. Thus, although the present inquiry may not yield any substantial generalities about the roles of science and technology in society, it is to be hoped that the conceptual tools forged in the pages which follow may be used to glimpse new insights and enrich our understanding of the complex matters at hand. If nothing else, the efforts presented in this text at least undermine the tenability of any simplistic truisms about the causal role of science and technology in society. And it is to be hoped that these meager insights will prove useful to anyone concerned with these topics, which should include everyone.

It is like the parable of the vintner who, as he lays dying, tells his sons of a treasure buried in his vineyard. After his death, his sons, in their efforts to uncover the treasure, till the vineyard thoroughly, providing the cultivation which yields a bumper crop.

References

1. Daniel Kevles, "Big Science and Big Politics in the United States: Reflections on the Death of the SSC and the Life of the Human Genome Project," Historical Studies in the Physical Sciences. 27 (2) 1997, pp. 269-270.

2. Kevles, p. 273.

3. Kevles, pp. 292-3.

4. Laplace, Pierre Simon, A Philosophical Essay on Probabilities, translated from the 6th French edition by Frederick Wilson Truscott and Frederick Lincoln Emory. (New York: Dover Publications, 1951), p.4.

EXERCISES

Multiple-Choice

_____ 1. Which of the following statement is true?

    a. Science should be studied in isolation, independently of all concerns external scientific activity.

    b. The developing relationship between technology and the society it is unimportant.

    • c. The historical interactions of science, technology, and society are complex, but studying these interactions provides a better understanding of contemporary issues in science, technology, and society.

    d. Citizens of a democratic nation have no influence over the development of science and technology.

_____ 2. Contingent coincidences are

    a. related events.

    • b. events or conditions which might just as well not be associated at all.

    c. events that are necessarily connected.

    d. like when a moving cue ball hits another ball and causes its motion.

_____ 3. Which of the following statements is false?

    a. Causality can be thought of in terms of cause and effect.

    b. In contingent coincidences, there is no necessity.

    c. Looking at how one event or condition causes another does not imply that there are not other events or conditions that could have led to the same effect.

    • d. By wearing a green shirt, John caused his friend's birthday to be June 15.

_____ 4. Natural laws

a. are written in organic ink,
b. express only contingencies,
. c. are true lawlike statements in the form "All objects that possess the property F also possess the property G" or "All F are G,"
d. express accidental relationships between events.

_____ 5. Which of the following statements are true?
a. Technological determinism is the belief that technology drives progress.
b. Progress is the idea that man can become more civilized.
c. Progress is an Enlightenment ideal.
d. (a) and (c)
e. All of the Above

True/False

_____ 1. SSC stands for Super Science Creator.
_____ 2. Understanding the complex relationships between science, technology, and society will help individuals become more informed citizens.
_____ 3. In his *Philosophical Treatise of Probabilities*, LaPlace envisioned a super-intellect, later referred to as "LaPlace's Demon," whose intelligence was so powerful that it could grasp the values of all the essential physical parameters of every particle in the universe in a given moment.
_____ 4. Technological innovation rests on scientific findings.
_____ 5. Necessity is the idea that if the antecedent event or condition occurred, the effect just had to follow.
_____ 6. Technological advance always produces social benefits.
_____ 7. Although the Industrial Revolution produced remarkable achievements, from the steamship, to the railroads, to the telegraph, it also yielded a plethora

of inexpensive goods, which acted as a palliative for the laboring masses.

_____ 8. Social benefits can be remedied by technological means.

_____ 9. The idea of "progress" only has to do with an accumulation of more, better material things.

_____ 10. The SSC was proposed as a technological aid to investigate some of the most fundamental questions in particle physics.

Discussion Questions

1.   What are some scientific discoveries that have occurred in your lifetime? How was technology involved in the discovery or in the implementation of the science? How have these discoveries changed our expectations of life?

2.   What are some technological advances that have occurred during your lifetime? What problems have these technologies proposed to fix? What problems have they created?

3.   Think about what you do from the time you wake up until you go to sleep. Consider even the most routine actions of your life: personal hygiene, eating, drinking, et cetera. In what specific ways does science determine what you do or don't do? In what specific ways does technology govern how you do what you do?

2

SCIENCE AND TECHNOLOGY: SOME FUNDAMENTALS

> Man, being servant and interpreter of Nature, can do and understand so much and so much only as he has observed in fact or in thought of the course of nature: beyond this he neither knows anything nor can do anything.
>
> -Francis Bacon, *Novum Organum*

The terms "science" and "technology" are used fluidly, in the sense that they are used to mean different things in different contexts. Sometimes these terms designate activities, like preparing specimens in a lab, running tests, or writing reports, all of which are sometimes collected under the heading of "science." Similarly, "technology" sometimes refers to the institutions supporting those activities, like universities or firms which are heavily invested in research, like Monsanto or Cargill. Sometimes "science" and "technology" are simply used to refer to the products or outcomes of these activities. In this sense, an article in a scholarly journal like *Nature* or *Science* might simply be called "science". Likewise, an iPod, a Smart Phone, or a laptop computer might simply be called "technology". In both cases, it is absolutely imperative to seek the broadest conception possible, so that we would include as science anything ranging from the speculations of pre-Socratic thinkers like Thales, who declared that everything was water, to the latest article in a top science journal. Similarly, an understanding of technology, if it is to yield any insight into the subject-matter, must be sufficiently broad to include, cheek-by-jowl with the electronic gizmos and gadgets of today,

Archimedes Screw Pump

historical technologies, like water mills or Archimedean screw-pumps, and even the twig stripped of bark that chimpanzees use to fish for termites. In all the cases that should be included—under science or technology—there must be an element of conscious intention on the part of their creator. There are animal behaviors that result in artifacts which seem very close to what are indisputably technologies, but which show no evidence of planning or forethought, like a wasp's nest or a beaver dam. Certainly no one would wish to attribute to their creators the kind of prescience so evident in human works. Yet there are

Chimp Eating Termites

other animal behaviors that seem just as intentional as the most carefully planned human accomplishments. So while there is certainly a sharp distinction between the instinctual behavior of animals burrowing, nesting, or building dams and the deliberate, mindful behavior of *homo sapiens* and his closest kin, there are bound to be borderline cases as well, which can only be decided by consensual decisions on a case-by-case basis.

.

The Aims of Science and Technology

Unsurprisingly, science and technology share many common traits but also differ in fundamental ways. One very useful way to capture what they share as well as how they differ is by considering their respective aims or goals. The identification of the aims of science and technology given below are offered only as starting-points for further discussion. At first glance, they seem to provide a deep and thorough-going division between the two but, as the discussion progresses, it will become clear that

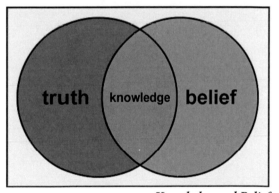

Knowledge and Belief

there are, indeed, areas of overlap, too. Taken in this spirit, they provide a useful beginning for the development of a fuller, more comprehensive understanding. At the same time, it will be possible to discover the limits of thinking of the respective aims of science and technology in this way.

The Aim of Science is to develop a body of knowledge which describes reality.

Philosophers since Plato have been discussing the nature of knowledge and, even though they have abandoned the effort to fully define it, they have determined that it must have certain necessary characteristics. For a belief—whether it is just a factual claim, a universal hypothesis, or a theory—to count as knowledge, it must be both *justified* and *true*. The first point worth noting is that knowledge is a body of belief possessing certain key characteristics, which distinguish it from other bodies of belief, including beliefs that are justified but mistaken, as well as ones that are made up out of thin air as well. Accordingly, philosophers have long agreed that knowledge is belief which is both justified and true. This is not a definition, but a minimal list of necessary features that a belief (or body of beliefs) must possess to qualify as knowledge. Of course, an important task for science is to set the terms by which beliefs are justified and to reach a consensus about which beliefs are more or less justified than others. Indeed, the criteria of justification may vary from science to science, so that the methods and standards employed in chemistry might well differ from those used in physics, say, or geology. Once it is agreed that a belief, or body of beliefs, satisfies the criteria of justification set by the practitioners of a particular discipline, the belief (or body thereof) is regarded, for all intents and purposes, as true, at least until challenged.

Of course, this is just to remind ourselves that there is no criterion of truth, no sure-fire method of determining -once and for all time, so to speak- which beliefs are true. So when a belief satisfies the standards prevailing in a given field, it is accepted as true, at least for the time being. Indeed, circumstances may arise in the future which would require re-visiting the matter but, until then, the belief is tentatively accepted as true.

This understanding of "knowledge" clarifies thorny cases which are sometimes presented to "stump" an audience. Typically, someone will provoke the "stumper" by some well-intentioned statement, like

We know that the earth is round.

The speaker will then be presented with a skeptical response, like "How do you know?" or "How can you be so sure?," followed up with the claim that it's not simply true that the earth is round but, rather, that even though it is known to be true *now*, it was not always. Indeed, it used to be that

It is known that the earth is flat,

implying that the very concept of knowledge is relative to different times, so that what was once knowledge may not be at another time. But this is a misunderstanding of an otherwise simple matter. Earlier it was believed—with some justification—that the earth is flat. But, in fact, the earth was not flat, not then, not ever. So the belief was not true. Hence, it was never *known* that the earth was flat; it was simply believed *incorrectly*. Or, in other words, even though it was accepted as knowledge because it satisfied the criteria for acceptance at that time, it was later discovered that it fell short of the standards after all.

Truth is understood as correspondence with reality, in the sense that the belief that Fido is a dog is true because the pet, Fido, is a member of a certain species, called "dog" in English. Notice, first of all, that there is no mention of whether anyone knows that Fido is a dog, so a belief can be true without anyone knowing it. For that matter, no one even has to believe that Fido is a dog. Understood this way, beliefs are the sort of thing expressed by a declarative sentence. Returning to the issue at hand, the aim of science as characterized above may be better understood when contrasted with the aim of technology:

> *The Aim of Technology is to employ justified beliefs, concerning organizational systems and artifacts, for achieving practical solution to concrete problems.*

The most significant difference between science and technology lies in their aims. While science is conducted in the pursuit of knowledge, technology is developed in order to achieve the more immediate, practical goal of solving concrete problems.

One important point of comparison between the aims of science and technology concerns the difference between knowledge and justified belief. It may seem like the difference implies that technology pursues a less significant goal than science. Nothing could be further from the truth. In fact, this consequence is a relatively superficial implication of the statements of the goals of science and technology.

Early Table Fan

The fundamental difference between science and technology emerges when the focus is shifted to the difference separating knowledge and justified belief. And that difference is just truth. So, since science is the pursuit of knowledge, it is the pursuit of justified belief which is true. In contrast, technology is the pursuit of justified belief that yields a practical solution to a concrete problem. In other words, the difference between science and technology is just the difference between truth and practicality. Truth is just about the relations between the way we think the world is and the way it is as a matter of fact. Truth is an all-or-nothing affair. A belief or statement is either true or false; there is no in-between. (In logic, this is known as "the law of excluded middle." The medieval logicians had a more graphic name for it, *"Tertium non Datur,"* which means — roughly—"there is no third alternative available.")

Thales of Miletus

The absolute, all-or-nothing character of truth contrasts sharply with the practicality of technology's goal. The aim of providing a practical solution to a concrete problem does admit of degrees, of more-or-less, of good-and-better. One of earliest electrical appliances was the oscillating fan, a table-top model which swiveled back and forth as it sent a cool breeze across a hot room on a sultry summer day. Available in the late 19th Century, early fans were little more than blades attached to an electric motor. Soon the blades were enclosed in a cage, to protect the expensive blades (rather than humans in the vicinity!). This device satisfied the aim of providing a practical solution to the summer heat. They worked fine and there are specimens from the 1920's that are still around—and in good working order. Despite the fact that they were a perfectly satisfactory remedy for the problem, they were soon displaced by home air conditioners, which began to appear around 1930. The succession of these two technologies, both addressed to relieve the same discomfort, shows that a solution to a problem maybe perfectly good while another solution to the same problem is even better. It is in precisely the fact that technologies admit of degrees that it differs from science in an essential way. Technologies are more or less, better

⅄ or worse but scientific theories, hypotheses, and statements are simply true or false. Or, as the medieval logicians would have said, *tertium non datur!*

Critical Questions

At this juncture, it is worth pausing briefly, in order to use the ideas about the aims of science and technology to reflect on what critical ideas emerge that would b e useful in assessing claims about science and technology in society. The first, and most obvious type of question to ask about any claim whatsoever -regardless of whether it concerns science, technology, or their interactions with technology- concerns their truth. After all, every claim, every statement, attempts to characterize the world and, if it is true, then that is the way the world is, as a matter of fact. So it is natural to ask, about any statement whatsoever,

What must the world be like if the statement is true?

This question can be understood, first of all, in terms of what the statement in question requires or assumes. If, for instance, the statement is "The present king of France is bald" it assumes, as a beginning, that there is presently a king of France. So "The present King of France is bald" assumes the truth of the statement, "There is a present king of France." If the assumption is true, then what else would be true if the statement were true? That is to say, what does the original statement imply or entail? Obviously, that the present king of

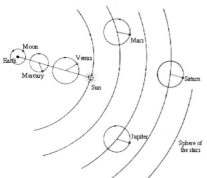

Ptolemy's Cosmos

France is hairless. This analysis was relatively simple, largely because further inquiry into the underlying assumptions of the

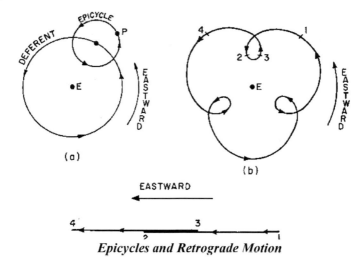

Epicycles and Retrograde Motion

statement in questions was limited. One might have pushed things further, inquiring (for instance) into the lineage of the present occupant of the throne in order to ascertain his legitimacy as king.

Obviously, the investigation of assumptions is, within limits, a rather pedestrian affair, requiring only the most trivial methods. But in some cases, more imagination is required and the challenge becomes more daunting - and more interesting, too.

The Pessimistic Meta-Induction ƤMI

The very idea that the aim of science is truth seems, at first blush, a bit "over the top," considering that the historical path of science is a trail littered with incorrect, mistaken, and out-and-out false beliefs. Beginning at the beginning, there was

Ptolemy's astronomical theory which placed the earth at the center of the planetary system, with the remaining five (yes, count them, five!) planets (including the sun) rotating around it on convoluted orbits on orbits on orbits. It is difficult indeed to begin to say what Ptolemy's biggest mistake was—perhaps the orbits on orbits (called "epicycles"), the number of the planets, missing the profound difference in kind separating the sun from the other heavenly orbs, or—(almost forgot!)—the stationary position of the earth at the center of the scheme. Even Copernicus' improvement, introduced in his book *On the Revolutions of the Heavenly Spheres* of 1543, retained the artifice of epicycles as well as the circular orbits passed down to him from antiquity.[1] Indeed, it might well be argued that it was Copernicus" attachment to the circularity of planetary orbits that motivated him to create a system in which the sun, rather than the earth, was positioned at the center.

Or, to shift to another field, what about Aristotle's idea that objects fell to earth because that was their "natural place?" Of course, the doctrine of natural place explains that, just as the natural place of water was on top of earth (including stuff composed mainly of earth), so the place of fire was above all the others. Consequently, earth falls through air (above water) and water to its natural place, and fire always rises. Just light a match and see whether the flame point up or down.[2]

Another favorite scientific misconception is phlogiston, originally conceived as the combustible part of "stuff." In other words, if you want to find out how much phlogiston is contained in a table, just weigh it, burn it, weigh the ashes, and take the difference

Anton Lavoisier

between the two weights. Phlogiston, in short, is whatever is burned off during combustion. Of course, phlogiston became one of the "dodos" of science when Antoine Lavoisier revolutionized chemistry with the discovery of oxygen in the 18th Century.[3] The ironic part of the story is that it was actually Joseph Priestley who made the discovery and who then communicated it to Lavoisier. But Priestley called the gas he produced "dephlogisticated air." Lavoisier recognized that what Priestley had discovered was, in fact, a more fundamental substance than its discoverer realized. So Lavoisier named it "oxygen" and built modern chemistry on its basis.

In short, the story of science is that of error after error after error. From this past record, some people have drawn the conclusion that, probably, current science is wrong, too. Today's scientists may not realize it, but their most cherished beliefs will, in a generation or two, go the way of the geocentric planetary scheme, the doctrine of natural place, or "phlogiston."

This train of thought—from the record of past scientific failures to the likely falsity of current belief—is sometimes called "the pessimistic meta-induction."[4] Of course, an induction is just the inference from a series of instances of a phenomenon, like

The 1st swan was white,

"   2d "

"   3d "

Therefore, all swans are white.

This line of reasoning leads from the repeated failures of scientific ideas in the past to the conclusion that all the hypotheses and theories proposed by science—not just past ones but present and future ones as well—will also turn out to be false. And, of

PMI

because Ptolomey is wrong, we have to scrap all the aspects of what he was saying. have to disagree with everything that they said if it failed course, it is the conclusion that is pessimistic simply because, if all scientific efforts to describe reality are destined to be false, then why bother at all?

The form of the argument is an induction, because it proceeds from particular premises to a general conclusion. Since the conclusion covers a potential infinity of cases, no collection of particular premises—no matter how large—can ever justify the inference to the conclusion. In other words, the conclusion says more than the content expressed by all the premises combined. And that's why inductive inferences are called "ampliative"— they amplify the information contained in their premises. The present argument, from the repeated failures of past science to the likely failure of present science, is actually a *meta-induction*, since it is *about* the history of science. But there's no reason why the pessimistic meta-induction cannot be turned on its head. Every failed scientific idea was succeeded by a better one, which did not turn out to be false (at least not in the respect in which its predecessor was). So if the history of science can be viewed as a train of failures, it can just as readily be regarded as an impressive string of advances, in which the best ideas science has to offer are always succeeded by even better ones. And therein lies scientific advance.

By the same token, there hardly seems to be anything wrong with offering a highly idealistic conception of science, especially when it is kept in mind that the practice of scientists is directed towards the acquisition of knowledge in precisely this ideal sense. Indeed, the only time scientists continue to work with theories they know are wrong, or have limitations, is when the theory at hand is otherwise largely successful, its successes can be isolated from its limitations, and there is no viable alternative available. It makes much more sense to proceed with a conception of reality that is broadly confirmed, even though it possesses minor limitations or errors in a restricted part of its domain of application, than to proceed with no idea at all.

One dramatic implication of the pessimistic meta-induction is that science, despite all its successes, its explanations of what seem to be utterly improbable phenomena, its predictions of the most unexpected outcomes, is frequently mistaken. Despite the best efforts of the most talented experimentalists and theoreticians, science still describes things falsely from time to time. In short, *science is corrigible* . . . which is hardly surprising since it is the creative product of human beings.

The discussions of the aims of science and technology given earlier emphasize the most important common features shared by science and technology, as well as the salient differences separating them: science and technology are both bodies of belief, manifested in quite different things and distinguished by quite different goals. After all, what the definitions highlight most dramatically is that science seeks to describe reality but technology is content with an understanding of nature which is adequate for making artifacts and devices to solve concrete problems. Clearly, science and technology have much in common: primarily that both are systems of belief and therefore require justification. More germane to present purposes are the differences between them and the principal one of these, as noted above, is that technology pursues practical goals external to the system of belief while science pursues the cognitive goal, judged by its own internal standards, of a true description of the world. Thus, science is understood as inquiry which pursues the cognitive goal of acquiring knowledge of reality. Technology, like science, is a system of beliefs. Since these beliefs do not need to be true to serve their purpose for the design and implementation of technology, does not, however, imply that they are not justified. Although the justification of many technologies is simply trial and error, these tests are just as legitimate as scientific experiments and, in more extreme cases, like weaponry and spacecraft, are given extensive preliminary testing prior to any trials which are expensive or involve human life. The key point is that, unlike science, technology is always an entirely pragmatic affair, the success of which can be judged in terms of its achievement of some practical end. (One might say it is conceived "instrumentally," in that technology—the artifacts and systems, not the activity—is conceived as a tool for a specific use.)

Another way the difference between science and technology becomes obvious is in the practice of scientists and engineers. When a technological solution to a practical problem is found, it is because the inventors of the technology have sufficiently justified their beliefs about the matter to make the artifact they were seeking. For the practical purposes at hand, their beliefs are sufficiently justified. But scientists are never satisfied. When they gather sufficient justification to regard their beliefs as the best explanation of the matters at hand, they continue to look for further justification. Indeed, since their pursuit is directed towards truth, they exert every effort to make sure that their explanation of the phenomenon at hand is the only possible one. So their investigation proceeds by eliminating all other possible sources of explanation, all other candidates for the honorific, "truth of the matter."

Alexander Graham Bell

It should be noted that, on this view, the success of a particular technology can only be judged relative to the task for which it was developed. Thus, automobiles should be assessed on their merits as personal vehicles, to be used within a limited range of circumstances. It would be unfair to regard cars as failures because they do not fly or float. At the same time, however, it should be kept in mind that some technologies succeeded and became widespread only when applied to some task their developers never anticipated. It is well known, of course, that Alexander Graham Bell envisioned the telephone as an entertainment device, which would provide the user with access to entertainments like symphony performances.[5] Similarly, Thomas Edison expected the principal use of the phonograph would be to record last wills and testaments.[6]

"Theories," "Hypotheses," and "Laws"

It should be mentioned that the beliefs which figure so largely in the conceptions of science and technology are typically formulated in statements which scientists and engineers commonly describe as "theories," "hypotheses," and "laws". These words are used rather loosely in technical contexts, though often non-scientists add connotations that no specialist would ever acknowledge.

Albert Einstein

For instance, one often hears phrases like, "That's the problem with evolutionary theory; it's just a theory!" Of course, this phrase is uttered in a tone of voice indicating that the speaker considers it a definitive refutation of evolution. Nonsense! For one reason, the modern theory of evolution is probably one of the most well confirmed beliefs in the entire history of science. Or consider another likely candidate, the General Theory of Relativity, proposed by Albert Einstein in 1916. Until just a few years ago, it was the most highly confirmed account of bodies in motion throughout the natural sciences since man first started gazing at the stars and wondering about them. Yet it was still called a "theory." Or consider the arithmetic of the positive integers, which mathematicians often refer to as "number theory." Could you imagine someone saying, "That's just the problem with arithmetic; it's really just number theory, and that's only a theory!"? (Of course, it would be even funnier if someone said this after adding incorrectly!) So beware misuses of the word "theory," especially ones that attach pejorative connotations that no scientist or engineer would ever accept.

In fact, anyone who uses "theory" with negative connotations is really equivocating, mixing two different meanings of the term, each of which is perfectly acceptable and useful in its own context. When a scientist or engineer calls some belief a "theory," they usually intend to indicate that they are describing something as a body of abstract beliefs, which unifies a domain of phenomena. But in everyday parlance, to call something a "theory" is to say it is highly speculative, more of a hunch, intuition, or guess, rather than a belief securely grounded in solid evidence. So when someone speaks derisively of an abstract body of scientific beliefs as a "theory," he is really playing on both of these meanings—talking out of both sides of his mouth, so to speak.

One important logical feature that all scientific theories have in common is that they are universal in form. That is to say, they concern absolutely everything, in any point of space-time whatsoever. Suppose that "F" and "G" are properties which material particles may or may not possess, as the case may be. For instance, "F" might be the property of being a heavy body and "G" might apply to all falling bodies. Then, if the letter "x" functions as a variable (just as in algebra) ranging over material things (like bodies or particles—unlike in algebra, where variables range over numbers), there might be a scientific theory which says

All x which are F are also G.

In other words, the fictional theory just says that absolutely every material thing which has the property F also has the property G. In the example, all heavy bodies fall. Of course, no scientific theory merely asserts some property universally of everything, for all kinds of reasons (for instance, it would be boring). Rather, theories typically restrict their scope to objects in a particular domain. And this is captured in the above statement by the use of a conditional form in which the domain of discourse is restricted to those things which possess the property F (or, in other words, satisfy the condition F). This is best expressed by representing theories as conditional statements of universal form, or universal conditionals. Then the universal conditional

> For every x, if x is an F, then x is a G,

says the same thing as the earlier statement. Or, in yet other words,

> Everything which is an F is a G,

or,

> All F's are G's [7]

Note specifically that it does not say that everything is either an F or a G or even, for that matter, that there are any F's or G's at all. It merely says that anything whatsoever which is an F— anything which satisfies the conditions of being an F—is also a G, or possesses the property signified by "G". This is somewhat easier to comprehend if thought of in terms of particular— rather than universal—conditionals. Particular conditionals may be used to express the relation between initial conditions and the result of processes which take place over time. Just think of "F" as descriptive of the initial conditions of some experiment, like "a virus is introduced to the growth in the petri dish," "a 2 kg ball is raised to 15 km," etc. And "G" as what is supposed to result from whatever processes are described, like "the virus infects all the growth medium in 2 days," "the ball falls such-and-such a distance in a certain period," and so forth. Then two examples of particular conditionals would be

> If a virus is introduced to the growth in the petri dish, then the virus infects all the growth medium in 2 days,

and

> If a 2 kg ball is raised to 15 km, then the ball falls such-and-such a distance in a certain period.

And it is statements like these universal conditionals which make up the meat and potatoes of contemporary science—as well as most of the substantive claims of everyday life.

What was said earlier of "theory" holds equally of "hypothesis." Often this term is used, especially by non-specialists, to indicate a mere hunch or a wild guess. But that is not always the case. In fact, scientists frequently call a belief an "hypothesis" which is not—in the layperson's terms—hypothetical at all. Indeed, there are statements which scientists call "hypotheses," which are, in fact, quite well-supported by data.

Curiously, there was a time in the history of science when scholars used the term "hypothesis" to protect themselves from accusations of heresy. During the later

Averroes

Middle Ages, a new interest in learning flowered as the first universities emerged. At about the same time, the works of many of the ancient Greeks, especially Aristotle, were first translated in their entirety into Latin. As scholars began to defend and articulate the claims made in these works, Church authorities eyed them suspiciously. Indeed, at the University of Paris, there was a group who apparently defended a Muslim understanding of Aristotle, developed by the Arab scholar Averröes. Etienne Tempier, the bishop of Paris at that time, regarded the Averröist interpretation as genuine Aristotelian doctrine. After a number of half-hearted attempts, he finally issued the Condemnation of 1277, forbidding scholars to embrace 219 propositions (or beliefs) that were thought to be characteristic of the Averröist version of Aristotle.[8] But no one let the Condemnation restrict their scientific investigations. Instead, they began to consider the condemned claims "hypothetically;" that is, as if they weren't asserting their truth. This allowed the claims to be considered—by working out their consequences and determining their observational predictions—without fear of censure. Indeed, scholarly investigations proceeded as if the bishop had said nothing at all!

A well-confirmed scientific claim is the Kant-LaPlace Hypothesis, which concerns the development of nebulae. This contention, which dates back to the turn of the 19th Century, was probably the very first scientific statement with a truly evolutionary component, for it concerned the development of stars over vast stretches of time. And today, physicists still regard it as accurate within certain limits. Since physicists also know what those limits are, it can still be used to make accurate predictions (within the range of its applicability). So even though it's perfectly useful, and true within certain limits, it's still called an "hypothesis." Or consider Georg Cantor's Continuum Hypothesis, which concerns the structure of (mathematical) infinity. In brief, it states that there are unequal infinite collections which are themselves structured in an infinite series. It cannot, in principle, be proven mathematically, so it's often adopted as an axiom which has proven extremely useful in studying the relations of infinite collections. But it's still called an "hypothesis." How can something be called an "hypothesis" as well as an "axiom?" Only because these terms, as scientists use them, are far more fluid and flexible than most people think.

The situation is similar with "laws." The natural supposition is that laws are the most highly regarded of scientific statements and, by definition, all laws are exceptionless. Thus it might seem that, when first proposed, a given scientific contention has the status of a theory or hypothesis and, as it is further and further confirmed through observation and experiment, it becomes accepted more and more by the community of practicing scientists until it achieves the status of a law, which means it is virtually unassailable. But there's a problem with this story. Most statements which are called "laws," especially in physics, are phenomenological, which is to say that they deal with directly observable phenomena. In fact, most laws date back to the days when science was concerned with identifying the regularities directly observable in nature, with little suspicion that these regularities might simply be the effects of unobservable, and as yet undiscovered, underlying causes. This is true of Newton's Laws, for instance, which concern the motions of celestial bodies as well as objects moving near the surface of the earth. (Like a ball tossed across the lawn by two people playing catch.) But with the advent of Relativity Theory and its confirmation within a few years, scientists learned that, strictly speaking, Newton's laws are false. Nonetheless, within certain limits, they are perfectly accurate and, perhaps because of their continuing usefulness, they're still called "laws." Certainly, Newton's laws are close enough for most practical (and many theoretical) purposes.

To reiterate, one needs to be as careful of the word "law" as one does of the words "theory" and "hypothesis." Laws in science are not sacrosanct edicts issued as true once and for all time. There are no certainties in science, and surely this includes what scientists call "laws". Indeed, one truth about science you can "take to the bank" is that, in science, nothing is sacrosanct. Any claim, no matter how long it has been held by the community of scientific practitioners, regardless of how well confirmed it is through experiments and observations, is susceptible to revision or outright abandonment. Science is a cruel mother, who gives birth to beautiful, promising babies, but will throw them into the street at the first sign of a problem.

But when scientists thoroughly test an hypothesis, repeatedly subjecting it to rigorous experimentation and it withstands every effort at disproof, a consensus forms as a greater and greater proportion of the scientific community comes to support the hypothesis. Then the hypothesis takes on a likelihood that both scientists and laypersons can consider reliable, despite its continuing corrigibility.

Historical Trends in the Relations of Science and Technology

One of the most pervasive and most misleading bits of conventional wisdom is the idea that technology is little more than the application of science. To begin with, it is difficult to tell what is meant by the term "application" which is extremely ambiguous, at least in this context. What "application" might mean is that if one begins with a scientific generalization—say, a law of nature—and applies it to a specific case, the result is a recipe for constructing a useful device of some sort or other. The suggestion seems to be that merely stipulating a particular value for the variables in a scientific generalization yields the description of a particular technology. Certainly, the truth of the statement

All F's are G's implies that, for any particular x,

If x is F then x is G.

But to suppose that this method might result in some useful technology is, on the face of the matter, absurd. After all, what reason could there be to believe that, even if randomly choosing a value for the variable in a true generalized statement did, indeed, describe a gadget one could produce, would it have any utility? But even if it is granted that the utility of a particular application of science must be independently established before it can be concluded that technology is just the application of science, there are still problems facing the conventional wisdom.

In the first place, science and technology have had little to do with each other throughout most of their history. In classical Greece, science and technology flourished but each developed along its own independent trajectory. After all, science began with Thales" proclamation that "everything is water," uttered about the same time that aqueducts were being dug through

Eupalinos Tunnel (550-520 B.C.)

hills, starting on opposite sides several miles apart, to carry water to Athens. Because of the precision of the building plan as well as the skill of the engineers directing the workers, the tunnels met in the middle, with remarkable accuracy. And it is to be noted that their achievement was possible despite their ignorance of the idea that "everything is water!"

Similarly, the Romans created some of the most remarkable technologies found in the ancient world. Among these, some of the most amazing were the aqueducts which carried fresh water to Rome, many of which are still standing today. Their military leaders adopted the phalanx formation from the Greeks but improved it by reducing the rows and ranks of soldiers. The result was a far more flexible—and much deadlier—formation. Roman engineers provided the best roads the ancient world had seen, as well as the strongest bridges and the first catapults. And one hardly needs to describe Roman achievements in architecture and construction which relied, for the first time in history, on the use of lime to make concrete. And, as for Roman science, it was virtually non-existent –apart from Lucretius" *On The Nature of Things*- and therefore contributed nothing to their technology.[9]

The Middle Ages witnessed a flourishing of technology, though this is often overlooked since it is forgotten that medieval civilization arose in formerly "barbarian" lands, with distinctive social structures, and in quite different material conditions. One salient difference in social structure was due to Christian beliefs that prohibited slavery and thus created the need to save labor. One immediate consequence was that production was soon based on energy sources besides manpower, thus accounting for the

Medieval Water Wheel

expanding use of water and windmills. Although watermills had been known in Roman times, they proliferated exponentially in the Middle Ages. Indeed, by the year 1200, there were already 70 mills located in the Seine in Paris and the *Domesday Book* reported in the 11ᵗʰ Century that there were more than 5000 watermills in England. The science governing the force of falling water would not, of course, become known until the 17th Century, when it was derived from Galileo's Laws.[10] Similarly, the invention of the ploughshare, so necessary for tilling the heavy soils of northern Europe, had no foundation in medieval science. For that matter, the horse collar, which provided a new source of animal power for the plows, was also a medieval development necessitated, in part, like the ploughshare, by the heavy, wet soils of northern Europe. And although the Middle Ages are not known for a plethora of new scientific results, it would be wrong to draw the conclusion that scientific activity was non-existent in the era. Indeed, with the rise of the universities beginning in the 11th Century, and the re-discovery of Aristotelian texts shortly afterwards, medieval science was well on its way towards providing, in the words of one historian, the very foundations for the modern science which emerged in the Scientific Revolution.[11]

These broad trends in different historical epochs, clearly establish the independence of scientific investigations and technological development, as their respective fortunes rose and fell regardless of how the other fared. Some would say that these historical examples show nothing significant about the relations of science and technology today. And it certainly does seem, to the lay spectator, that science drives technological advance in the contemporary milieu. A quick glance at the biographies of many of the pioneers of the digital revolution would, however, reveal a quite different story. Few were scientists, in any sense of the word. Certainly, few had advanced scientific training and, for that matter, not many of them completed an undergraduate curriculum. Like so much of technology, the digital revolution was the result of very clever and very innovative but not very well trained individuals, working with others just like them.

Technological Stimulation of Science

Further evidence that the connection between science and technology is not the simplistic linear relation alleged by the conventional wisdom is provided by the numerous cases in which the direction of influence was the exact opposite. For there are countless historical incidents when, in fact, scientific advancement was stimulated by efforts to develop technology or by technology already developed.

One of the classic instances of a scientific advance triggered by a technological development was Galileo's use of the telescope to observe the night sky and discover evidence for the Copernican hypothesis. Galileo had long been convinced by Copernicus' treatise that the sun was the center of the planetary system. At the time, however, there was no convincing observational evidence which would conclusively establish the superiority of heliocentrism. In 1609, Galileo heard that a novel device, consisting of a tube that made objects at a distance appear larger, was the latest fad sweeping Amsterdam. Galileo's genius immediately realized the scientific potential of the "spyglass," as well as the basic optical principles underlying its operation, and he immediately wrote out instructions for the

Evangelista Torricelli and his Barometer

production of lenses. Within a few days, he had constructed the first telescope for astronomical observations and turned it towards the night sky. His observations included the craters on the moon, the phases of Venus, and the moons of Jupiter, which he first reported to the public in his book, *Siderius Nuncius,* or "The Starry Messenger."[12] Galileo's evidence ushered in a wholly new epoch in science by relying, for the first time in history, on observations made with the assistance of an instrument, a technology which greatly extended the range of human perception.

Another example, drawn from the Scientific Revolution, was the discovery by Torricelli—a student of Galileo—of the weight of air, while working to improve the air-pump, a technological device used primarily for experiments on the vacuum.[13] But perhaps the most well-known example in which a technological development spurred a scientific one is provided by the invention of the live steam injector by Henri Giffard in 1858. The injector used steam to lift fresh water from a tank to replenish the water in the boiler of a steam engine. The prevailing scientific conception of heat, the caloric theory, implied that the injector came dangerously close to a perpetual motion machine. This would be the same thing, according to one engineer, as if "a man could raise himself by pulling on his bootstraps." According to an alternative— but less accepted—understanding of heat, the kinetic theory, the injector converted heat to energy, with appropriate losses in the transfer. Although Giffard himself was familiar with both the caloric and the kinetic theories, neither one proved useful in guiding his design. Once the design was completed, however, the superiority of the kinetic theory became apparent to a larger and larger proportion of the scientific community.[14] Finally, the celebrated French scientist, Henri Poincarè, explained the operation of the injector by means of the laws of Thermodynamics in 1908.[15]

Even as science began to make greater contributions to

technological innovation in the 19th Century, its role was limited to rather basic and somewhat dated material. In the iron and steel industry, a major transformation was brought about by the reductions in cost effected by the Bessemer process. Bessemer himself was wholly untutored in chemistry. Nor, for that matter, did his contemporaries have much of an idea of the chemical nature of the processes occurring in a Bessemer converter. In fact, when first tried in Britain, the Bessemer process failed. Actually, the Bessemer innovation of injecting air into molten iron only removed the carbon and silicon impurities, not the phosphorous. But this was unknown because the process had only been tried previously with ores naturally bereft of phosphorous. In short, the Bessemer process only worked with a certain narrow ranges of naturally occurring ores. One result was that an economic advantage was automatically conferred on geographic areas endowed with non-phosphoric ores, like the Cumberland–Furnes region in Britain. Actually, Bessemer's original experiments were performed with highly pure pig iron from Sweden. Eventually, the use of Bessemer's process created a need for chemical analysis of the ores being used, as repeated failures of the process continued to occur. In fact, Bessemer's process eventually lost popularity as more advanced chemical analysis revealed that it not only reduced impurities, but introduced new ones, particularly nitrogen which made the resulting steel brittle.[16] Because of developments in the steel industry, basic chemical analysis eventually became more important as the economic advantages to be derived from a basic knowledge of chemistry yielded huge pay-offs. To the extent that technological advance depended on scientific results, these results were of the most rudimentary sort.

By the 20th Century, as some sciences became more directly linked to the development of technology, the relationship resembled more and more the linear connection imagined by the conventional wisdom. Still, study after study from the later

technology comes first sometimes. like with the telescope

20th Century indicates that much basic science proceeds with little or no regard for its technological application so that, if it ever does result in any technological development, it is many years later.

In recent decades, in a few but increasingly significant domains, the pursuits of science and technology have nearly fused. This merging of scientific and technological inquiry—as exemplified in recent bio-medicine, semiconductor electronics, and nanotechnology—promises to permanently change the understanding of science and technology, and their interaction with social forces. Indeed, the emergence of technoscience is the natural consequence of efforts to develop technology which, it turns out, depends on fundamental scientific results which have not yet been established. Thus technological advance—whether it is a cancer cure, an advanced electronic communication device, or a new application of carbon nanofibers--turns to basic research and the two co-develop symbiotically. Whether the combination of cognitive and practical goals typified by technoscience will remain limited to a few areas or will eventually dominate all domains of inquiry, requires a kind of speculation about the future which must be postponed until another day.

References

1.   Arthur Hyman and James J. Walsh. *Philosophy in the Middle Ages.* (Indianapolis: Hackett Company, 1973), pp. 582-591.

2.   Lucretius. *On the Nature of Things.* Anthony M. Esolen, trans. (Baltimore: Johns Hopkins University Press, 1995).

3.   Terry S. Reynolds. *Stronger than 100 Horses.* (Baltimore: Johns Hopkins University Press, 1983). Ch. 4.

4.   Ed Grant. *The Foundations of Modern Science in the Middle Ages.* (Cambridge: Cambridge University Press). pp. 80-83.

5.   Galileo Galilei. *Siderius Nuncius or The Sidereal Messenger.* Albert van Helden, trans. (Chicago: University of Chicago Press, 1989).

6.   W. E. Knowles Middleton. *The History of the Barometer.* (Baltimore: Johns Hopkins University Press, 1964). Ch. 2.

7.   Eda Fowlks Kranakis, "The French Connection: Giffard's Injector and the Nature of Heat," *Technology and Culture* 23 (1982), pp. 3-38.

8.   Henri Poincari, *Thermodynamique Cours de physique mathematique de la faculte des sciences de Paris,* 2d ed. (Paris, 1908), pp. 323-35.

9.   Nathan Rosenberg, "The Role of Science in the Innovation Process, 1860-1914," in Gustaf Berhhard, ed. *Science, Technology, and Society in the Time of Alfred Nobel.* (Oxford: Pergamon Press, 1982). Pp. 231-246.

EXERCISES

Multiple-Choice

_____ 1. Philosophers have argued that, at a minimum, knowledge consists of beliefs that are both _____ and true.
   a. correct
   b. specific
   c. justified
   d. testable

_____ 2. The aim of science is cognitive in nature, while technology strives towards _____ goals.
   a. economic
   b. selfish
   c. pragmatic
   d. down-to-earth

_____ 3. Beliefs are corrigible; they are always potentially mistaken and, accordingly, _____.
   a. changeable.
   b. meaningless.
   c. dangerous.
   d. blasphemous.

_____ 4. Statements of theories, hypotheses, and laws share two logical features: they are both universal   and
   _____.
   a. absolute.
   b. interrogatives.
   c. conjunctions.
   d. conditional.

_____ 5. Which of the following is **false**?
    a. Universal conditionals are conditional statements of universal form.
    b. The universal conditional "All men are mortal" implies that "Fido is mortal".
    c. Universal conditionals follow the form, "For every x, if x is an F, then x is a G."
    d. Theories are usually expressed in the form of a universal conditional.

True/False

_____ 1. The primary goal of modern medicine is technological, since its principal aim is to develop cures and treatments, seeking the underlying causes of these ailments only when necessary to develop an effective remedy.

_____ 2. Science may sometimes employ theories known to be flawed or to be limited when no better alternative is available.

_____ 3. In technoscience, the distinction between science and technology becomes blurred as technological advances co-develop with scientific discoveries.

_____ 4. Believing that currently accepted science will turn out to be false on the basis of past errors is called "the pessimistic meta-induction."

_____ 5. Lavoisier's discovery of oxygen confirmed the Theory of Phlogiston.

_____ 6. In the Middle Ages, science and technology were closely linked.

_____ 7. An important task for science is to set the terms by which beliefs are justified and to reach a consensus about which beliefs are more or less justified than others.

_____ 8. Bessemer used his background in chemistry to invent
the Bessemer Process.

_____ 9. Torricelli discovered the weight of air while improving
the air-pump.

_____ 10. Galileo had no contact with Copernicus.

Discussion Questions

1.   What do you think is the most beneficial scientific
discovery of the 20th century? Be sure you know the details of
the discovery, and can justify your answer.

2.   What do you think is the most beneficial technological
advance of the 20th century? What do you think is the most
harmful technological advance of the 20th century? Again, be
sure you know the details of the advancements, and can justify
your answers.

3.   To confirm you understand the universal form
of theories, make up your own example of a true theory
that clearly defines "x," "F," and "G," and is in the form of a
universal conditional. Your example can be as simple or as
complex as you"d like.

4.   As discussed, there are many historical examples
of how science and technology have developed separately.
Why do you think science and technology have become
more closely linked—so much so that we need a term for
it, "technoscience"—in the recent past? Based on this, what
predictions can you make about the future of science and
technology?

- Beliefs are expressed in declarative sentences
- a true belief describes the way things are

Justification of Beliefs. consists of evidence for/against claim

2 components: logic & observation
reasoned skills that can be & experience
learned

3

METHODS

> All things must be examined,
> debated, investigated without
> exception and without regard
> for anyone's feelings....

> -Denis Diderot, *Encylopedie*

The most important feature shared by science and technology,

J. M. Waterhouse' The Crystal Ball

as represented in the definitions given earlier, is that they are both systems of belief that are justified. Taking a close look at what counts as justification and how justification is related to beliefs is important for any number of reasons.

In the first place, it is essential to understand how scientists and engineers come to recognize the worth of the ideas that are key to their understanding of the world. It would, of course, be exciting and interesting to understand how scientists and engineers come to the creative insights, which resolve the mystery of an unexplained phenomena or provide the key to unlock some practical problem. This Eureka! Moment might come as the result of a reflective moment, in which a thinker escapes the nitty-gritty of pressing problems to serenely contemplate

some abstraction or even a beautiful vista. Or it might come during an instant of focused attention, directed towards the problem at hand. Whatever the circumstance,

Laboratory Scientist

understanding creativity has little bearing on the present goal, the development of a critical perspective of science and technology.

It is, however, germane to the aim of these efforts to grasp how scientists and engineers establish the value of their ideas, once they have occurred, the creative flash has passed, and the hard work of determining the worth of their insights confronts the scientist or engineer. It is at this point that the most difficult challenge occurs, not only for the investigator but also for the non-specialist anxious to understand the process of applying creative insights to concrete reality. For scientists, the challenge

Engineer at Work

might be in the form of some phenomena which has yet to be explained. For engineers, the challenge might be the device or gadget which solves some concrete practical problem. For the outsider, the spectator anxious to comprehend and evaluate the claims and promises made on behalf of scientific and technological developments and advances, it is how specialists apply their understanding that is the essential element in any critical understanding. And this understanding, this perspective on science and technology is a necessary prelude to the further goal of comprehending how technical endeavors interact with society.

And there are other, even more important incentives for examining inferential processes. Another, equally valuable lesson can be drawn from learning the ins and outs of the justification of beliefs. The study of science and technology in society may not, as a discipline, belong to the sciences or one of the fields of engineering. But any field of study, deserving of respect, will adhere to the same high principles of reasoning that prevail in the sciences and other technical fields. And so, too, must the standards of reasoning prevailing in the investigation of the relations among science, technology, and society be just as rigorous as in any other discipline. Studies in science, technology, and society must be just as demanding as botany, mathematics, or mechanical engineering.

Belief

At the core of any investigation about inferences and their correctness lies the notion of a belief. First of all, it should be noted that, in this context, nothing very technical is intended by "belief." In fact, it would be fine, for present purposes, to simply regard beliefs as the sorts of things that are expressed by declarative sentences. Thus, there are beliefs that

> Snow is white,
> The Boston Red Sox beat the Brooklyn

Robins in the 1916 World Series,

and

The economy will grow by 11.3%
next year.

One could go further and say that the belief expressed by the first sentence is also expressed (though in German) by

Schnee ist weiß.

And a true belief is just one that describes the way things, in fact, are. But that involves nothing more complicated than recognizing that it is a true belief that snow is white (even though it is summer right now and there is no snow), that the Boston Red Sox beat the Brooklyn Robins in the 1916 World Series (even though no one remembers the Brooklyn Robins), or that the expansion of the economy will be an impressive 11.3% (regardless of the fact that there will be no way to actually determine this for a year or more to come).

What is most important about truth is that there is a world of difference between the truth of a belief and our knowledge that it is true. For instance, if someone believed, back in 1929, that there were mountains on the far side of the moon, his belief

Lunar Surface

would be true, despite the fact that it would be nearly 40 years before anyone could justify that particular belief. Since he could not possibly have any justification for the belief, it would not count as knowledge. (In fact, we would probably just consider it "hot air!") This will be clearer once justification has been discussed.

Justification of Beliefs

Justification, in both science and technology, consists of two components, logic and observation, which is just to say that justification is both rational and empirical. Before introducing these concepts, it is worth taking a moment to distinguish proper justification from motivation, anecdotes, and autobiography.

Everyone recognizes that beliefs are not justified on the basis of what a psychic sees in a crystal-ball, his/her dreams, or visions one beholds when spiritually inspired. Rather, justification must consist of evidence for or against a claim, which is, strictly speaking, logically related to the claim. Although it is the burden of this chapter to discuss the detailed connections which logically link claims with their warrant, it is important to see that the roots of the current understanding of these matters lie with rather mundane, everyday intuitions. For instance, suppose the claim in question is simply:

1. Snow is white.

Clearly, good evidence for the truth of this claim might be:

2. When I looked out the window an hour ago, it was snowing, and the snow appeared white,

But the unrelated claims

> 3. I was brought up to believe that snow
>   is white,

or

> 4. It makes me feel warm and snuggly to
>   believe that snow is white,

do not increase the credibility of (1) at all. Of course, the reason why anyone would accept (2) as evidence, justification, or warrant for (1), while the very suggestion that (3) or (4) count as grounds for believing (1), is simply that (2) is logically connected to (1), but (3) and (4) are not. The salient fact that explains why neither (3) nor (4) could count as justification for (1) is that their truth has nothing to do with the truth of (1). Whether or not snow is white has nothing to do with your upbringing or how you feel. Certainly generations have been raised on false beliefs. Nor do one's feelings about a particular belief have any bearing on its truth. The fact is that the most erroneous beliefs may provide the kind of comfort and security people seek. Indeed, feelings—including feelings of certainty— would provide a poor guide indeed for wending one's way through the forest of claims and counter-claims that constitute popular culture.

There are, in fact, two distinct ways in which a claim offered as justification may count for the truth of some other claim, as direct observational evidence or as justification, which is inferentially related to the claim. It is the purpose of this chapter to provide an introduction to the kinds of logical relations that relate evidence to the claims they justify by briefly describing the kinds of relations studied in logic.

Justification of Reasoning
1. Bottom up
2. from the top down
3. comparison/this is like that

Types of Arguments

The proper object of study in logic is the argument. In this context, "argument" does not mean a heated exchange or the sort of discussion often held by friends or lovers just before they part paths forever. Arguments are to be regarded abstractly, as simply strings or sequences of statements.

In this context, a statement should also be regarded abstractly, as what is expressed by a declarative sentence, the kind of thing that can be true or false or the sort of conceptual structure used to express a belief. Then, of course, the same statement can be expressed by different declarative sentences, just as "Mary hit John" and "John was hit by Mary," say the same thing, even though they are quite obviously different sentences. Moreover, the same statement can be expressed in two different languages, just as "It is raining," "Il pleut," and "Es regnet" say the same thing in English, French, and German (respectively). So statements, thus conceived, are abstract entities, not the kind of things one can see and touch, like material objects such as tables, chairs, and written sentences.

In an argument, statements function either as premises or as conclusions. One should regard the premises as reasons offered to justify the conclusion or, in other words, grounds for the truth of the conclusion. Another way to say the same thing is just to say that one can infer the conclusion from the premises that an inferential relation holds between premises and conclusion.

In evaluating an argument, it is not the actual truth or falsity of the conclusion, or even the premises, that is important but how they "hang together" (so to speak), which distinguishes the good arguments. Indeed, it is the relations between premises and conclusion, the inferential relations that hold between the premises and conclusion of an argument that are of interest here.

Arguments come in two kinds: deductive and statistical. In a deductive argument, the premises purport to guarantee, warrant, or insure the truth of the conclusion. Statistical arguments, on the other hand, show only the probability the premises confer on the conclusion. For that matter, they may not necessarily even indicate that the premises make the conclusion likely. To get a taste of the

Lawnmowing

difference between these different types of arguments, consider the following examples:

1. 97% of all those who eat chocolate experience a feeling of euphoria.
   John ate a chocolate candy bar.

   _____

   Therefore, John will experience a feeling of euphoria.

2. All persons exposed to an atomic bomb blast at a distance of ten miles have an increased risk of cancer of 2%.
   Bill was exposed at a distance of ten miles to an atomic bomb blast.

   _____

   Bill is more likely to develop cancer.

3. Whoever mows the lawn will be paid $20.
   Marcus is mowing the lawn.

   _____

   Marcus will be paid $20.

Which conclusion are you most willing to believe, on the basis of the premises offered? In other words, supposing the premises—the first two statements in each of the foregoing triplets—are true, which is the most solidly founded conclusion? Obviously, the conclusion of (3). Indeed, if the premises of (3) are true, then the conclusion must be, as well. And that is because (3) is a deductive argument and a good one or, as logicians say, (3) is a valid deductive argument. (1) and (2), as indicated by the mention of probabilities, are statistical arguments. And anyone would be more likely to believe (1) than (2), simply on the basis of the fact that the probability of experiencing euphoria after eating chocolate is greater than the probability of developing cancer after exposure to an atomic bomb blast (at a distance of ten miles).

Arguments, as they occur in everyday discourse, are sometimes easier to analyze if they are first transposed into standard form, which is just a pattern that makes it simpler to identify the components of an argument. There's nothing mysterious about the idea of the standard form of an argument. It is simply a matter of putting the premises first to emphasize that the reasoning proceeds from premises to conclusion. In standard form, (3) becomes

> All persons who mow the lawn are persons who receive $20.
>
> All persons identical to Marcus are persons who mowed the lawn.
>
> _____
>
> All persons identical to Marcus are persons who receive $20.

In standard form, the premises are always listed first and the conclusion last; in this version, a line was added to clearly separate the conclusion from the premises. Admittedly, this transposition seems unnecessarily cumbersome, especially when you consider that what was actually said probably went like this:

> Hey! Any dude who mows the lawn gets $20 and that dude Marcus done it. So he gets the sawbuck!

Transposing arguments into standard form emphasizes the inferential relations between premises and conclusions which are, after all, of primary interest.

Of course, the formulation of (1) above is still unsatisfactory, because there is no mention of the fact that its inferential relation is probabilistic or that the conclusion only follows from the premises with a certain probability. But (1) might be fixed by putting it in this standard form:

> 97% of all persons who eat chocolate are persons who experience a feeling of euphoria.
>
> All persons who are John are persons who ate a chocolate candy bar.
> _____ [97%]
> All persons who are John are persons who will experience a feeling of euphoria.

Hershey's Addict

Here the double-lines clearly indicate that the argument is statistical rather than deductive, that the conclusion follows only probabilistically from the premises. Setting out the probability in brackets to the right of the double-lines emphasizes the strength (i.e., 97%) of the inference relation from premises to conclusion. There are other types of statistical arguments discussed in what follows, but the immediate goal is just to indicate, in a rough and ready way, the principal differences between deductive and statistical arguments.

Deductive Validity

Logically speaking, the best kind of deductive argument is a valid one, and a valid deductive argument is defined as an argument in which the truth of the

David's The Death of Socrates

premises guarantees the truth of the conclusion. That is to say, a valid argument is one in which, if the premises are true, the conclusion must also be true. Note that this is not to say that, in a valid argument, the premises are in fact always true. The definition merely states what would be the case if the premises were true. To take a simple example, consider the argument:

4. a) All men are mortal.
   b) Socrates is a man.

   ●────────────●

   c) Therefore, Socrates is mortal.

Remember that the single line between (b) and (c) indicates that the argument is offered as a deductive one, i.e., the truth of its premises are supposed to offer a compelling guarantee of the truth of its conclusion. And if (a) and (b) are taken as premises, and (c) as conclusion (indicated by the word "therefore"), (4) is clearly a valid argument. After all, if (a) and (b) are true, (c) must certainly be true as well.

Recall that the definition of validity given earlier does not require that the premises are, indeed, true; it merely specifies the truth-value of the conclusion when the premises are true.

Thus, deductive validity does not deal directly with truth (or, for that matter, falsehood) but, rather, the relations of possible truth and falsehood. Another way of putting it is to say that the validity of (4) does not depend on the particular concepts involved (i.e., men, mortality, and Socrates). Those particular concepts are, so to speak, incidental to the question of validity. Undeniably, these concepts are essential to the argument's content, but the validity of an argument has nothing to do with its content, with what the argument is about.

Any argument of the same form, i.e., the same arrangement of properties, is also valid, regardless of whether the premises or conclusion are, as a matter of fact, true.

Consider this permutation of (4):

> 5. a) All dogs are mortal.
>   b) Socrates is a dog.
>
> _____
>
>   c) Therefore, Socrates is mortal.

Since (5) is constructed by systematically substituting "dogs" for "men" in the premises of (4), both (4) and (5) have the same form. Thus, substituting these concepts affects only their content. Since validity is a property of arguments dependent on their form alone it follows that, if (4) is valid, so is (5). Even though premise (5b) is patently false, this does not bear on the validity of the argument. Validity is a property, which arguments possess (or not) regardless of the actual truth of their premises or conclusion. To reiterate, validity is about the relation between premises and conclusion, not about their factual truth.

Do the premises (5a) and (5b) lead to the true conclusion (5c)? They don't! Validity, after all, is a property of arguments, which tells us what happens when the premises are true. It doesn't tell us anything about the truth or falsity of the conclusion when the premises are false. So the truth of (5c) has nothing to do with the truth (or falsity) of (5a) and (5b).

In short, a valid argument with false premises gives no assurance, in itself, of anything whatsoever about the truth or falsity of the conclusion! In particular, the validity of an argument does not tell us that, when one or more of the premises are false, the conclusion will be, too. If, as things turn out, the conclusion is, in fact, true, it's not because of its relation to the premises. It's just a fluke! Another way of putting matters is to say that the validity of an argument concerns only one particular combination of truth-values of its premises and conclusions. Validity tells us that it is impossible for the premises to be true and the conclusion false. Validity says nothing about any other combination of truth-values in a valid argument.

Conditionals

Of course, science abounds with arguments, most of them valid though, surprisingly, one comes across some invalid ones. Although any comprehensive treatment of science would want to draw on the best examples, it turns out that some of the episodes in the history of science when invalid arguments repeatedly occurred are interesting for that very reason.

Here's one. Aristotle, the father of logic (!), reasoned that:

> If the earth were round, then the horizon
> would appear curved.
>
> The horizon does, in fact, appear curved.
> _____
>
> Therefore, the earth is round.

In Aristotle's argument, both premises and conclusion are true, though the argument is invalid. Why? Because the curved appearance of the horizon could be evidence of other things besides the roundness of the earth. For instance, if the earth were a flat disk, and not round, the horizon would appear curved nonetheless. In other words, the second premise would be true, but the conclusion would—if the earth were a disk—be false.

To see what's wrong with Aristotle's reasoning, suppose this statement appeared on a course syllabus:

> If anyone misses more than three classes,

> they will not receive an "A."

Statements of the form:

> If _ _ _, then . . .

are called "conditionals" or "hypotheticals." The first portion, the " _ _ _" following the "if," is called the "antecedent;" it states a condition that is sufficient for the latter part of the statement, the " . . ." part following the "then," which is called the "consequent."

It should be noted that this form may be either universal, like

> All ravens are black,

or particular, like

> The raven in the tree is black.

To call a statement a conditional is only to describe its form. It says nothing about its quantity, or the number of things to which it applies.

What happens when the antecedent is not fulfilled, when it is not true? Just suppose the statement on the syllabus strikes fear in the heart of every student in the class, and no one is absent on more than three occasions. In this case, the antecedent is clearly false. But what about the whole conditional? The entire statement is still true, even though the antecedent is false. (Nor does this mean that just being in class, and not missing more than three classes, is a guarantee of an "A"!)

One can argue all day about whether, indeed, this is what speakers of English intend when they use the "if . . ., then _ _ _" form of speech. And many logicians would agree that the logical parsing of this form as described above does not really capture the English expression at all. But, at least for present purposes, this is irrelevant. This understanding of "if . . ., then . . ." is good enough for the purposes of science, and it's incredibly simpler than any of the proposals that have been made to more accurately represent the way this expression is actually used in everyday discourse. So, for the sake of simplicity, one tolerates a little artificiality.

A true "if . . ., then _ _ _" statement says nothing about what happens when the antecedent is not fulfilled. This is essentially what happens in a valid argument. A valid argument only says what is the case under the condition that the premises are fulfilled (or true). A valid argument leaves open the question of what happens when the premises are false. And a conditional statement says nothing about what follows when the antecedent is not fulfilled. Of course, conditional statements arise frequently in science, and there will be ample opportunity to discuss them more later.

(As for the question of how Aristotle, the originator of logic, could have made such a mistake, the answer is simply that the logic he developed was not sufficiently powerful to deal with conditional statements. It had other shortcomings as well, and these failures were only overcome by the development of modern logic in the late 19th Century, by the mathematician, Gottlob Frege and the philosopher Bertrand Russell.)

Unlike the logician, scientists and engineers are more interested in the truth of statements than the inferential relations of statements in arguments. Of course, they also wish to avoid mistakes in reasoning, but they are, nonetheless, primarily interested in sound arguments: valid arguments that have true premises. That is to say, an argument is sound when it is valid and its premises are true.

Bertrand Russell

Of course, that is just the difference between the arguments (4) and (5). In the first argument, both the premises (4a) and (4b) are true, but the premise (5b) in the second argument is false. Thus, although both (4) and (5) are valid, (4) is sound while (5) is not. And, as noted earlier, the conclusion of a valid argument with one or more false premises may or may not be true. It also follows, from the definitions of validity and soundness, that the conclusion of any sound argument must also be true.

Logical Independence

One further matter of a logical nature, more essential to a spectator's understanding of science and technology than their internal workings, concerns independence, which is a logical property possessed (or not) by two (or more) statements. It is important because, in assessing the relations of scientific ideas, we often want to know whether or not we have to accept one to accept the other or if, instead, accepting one involves no commitment to the other.

The fact that independence is seldom understood or appreciated is appalling, for it is very straightforward. Suppose a given scientist defends two ideas, represented by "P" and "Q," which we may regard simply as statements. But suppose, further, that you agree with him that P is true though you have misgivings about Q. You are naturally led to the question whether you could, logically, accept P without also endorsing Q. And that is to raise the question whether Q is logically independent of P. But what, precisely, does this mean, and how do you find out?

Of course, to say that Q is dependent on P is just another way of saying P is sufficient for Q, or

> if P, then Q,

which, in turn, means that the deductive argument,

> P
> _____
>
> Therefore, Q,

is valid.

But then the question of independence becomes that of whether, in every conceivable case in which P is true, Q must also be true. If there is some possible situation in which P holds, but Q does not, then the argument is invalid and, accordingly, Q does not depend upon P.

But that is only half the story. For it may be the case that in every possible situation in which P is true, Q is false. Then the argument

> P
> _____
>
> Therefore, not-Q

is valid (where "not-Q" just signifies the opposite, or the negation, of Q). But if Q were logically independent of P, then P would have no influence whatsoever over the truth or falsity of Q. And that is just to require that the immediately preceding argument, like the earlier one, is invalid. Then, of course, it would not be the case that

P implies not-Q.

How would one go about showing that this statement is false? Simply conceive some circumstance, real or imaginary, so long as it is sufficiently plausible, in which P is true but not-Q is false, i.e., one in which both P and Q are true. Then, given that P does not imply Q nor does it imply not-Q, the truth of P has no influence over whether Q is true or false. And that just means that a statement Q is logically independent of P whenever both

P implies Q

and

P implies not-Q

are false. That is just to say, the truth of P tells us nothing about either the truth or falsity of Q; in short, Q is independent of P.

To return to the example of a scientist wondering whether defending P compels her to defend Q, the question is one of logical independence. And cases where the independence of ideas becomes extremely important abound in science and technology.

An example arose a couple of decades ago in evolutionary biology concerning the rate of species change, or speciation. Darwin proposed, in *The Origin of Species*, that evolution gradually, as entire species developed new characteristics, or major populations of a species became transformed, over long periods of time, into distinct species. Generations of biologists accepted Darwin's belief that species evolve gradually, through the occurrence of small mutations, incremental changes, which add up to a dramatic change resulting in a new species. Two theorists, Niles Eldredge and Stephen Jay Gould, challenged the gradualism in the received view of evolution. Instead, they proposed that evolution happened on a shorter time scale (though it still took millions and millions of years), they  argued that the fossil record supports the idea that new species appear when a population of an established species becomes geographically isolated from the parent population. In a small population, advantageous mutations spread rapidly, soon transforming the population into a new species. Eldredge and Gould's punctuated equilibrium model of evolutionary change is now accepted throughout the community of professional biologists. What is significant about this example is that it turns on questioning the independence of two statements:

> Species evolve,

and

> Speciation is a gradual, incremental process.

Before their work, neither Darwin nor any later biologists even raised this question. Yet the recognition of the independence of evolution and rate of speciation was the key to the development of a new model of evolutionary change.

Statistical Arguments

Mark Twain used to say, "There are three kinds of lies: lies, damned lies, and statistics" to criticize the use of statistical considerations to provide a semblance of strength to weak arguments. And there's clearly another sense in which what Twain said might also be true. And that is because most people have such a minimal grasp of statistics, or statistical studies in science, that they cannot even tell when they are being misled.

Mark Twain

Of course, no one actually reads the scholarly publications of professional scientists, where they provide all the detailed information necessary to judge the strength of a statistical finding (if one knew how). More likely, when the study has widespread effects on the population at large, one is more likely to find a report of the study in the popular press, like a newspaper or magazine. If a report of a test on a new drug said that 75% of all those who took the drug recovered from whatever ailment it is supposed to cure, you would naturally think that drug was promising, though you might continue to look for something better. But would you even consider the drug if you knew that, in the study reported, the drug was only administered to four people? Then it would appear that the results might be just a lucky role of the dice. So, for starters, one thing you would want to know about any statistical study is the size of the sample population.

Before turning to other features of statistical studies, which are helpful in assessing their merit, it is important to know that causal studies are of three basic types.

The first is an _experimental study_, in which a population is divided into the control group, consisting of individuals who will not be exposed to the suspected causal agent, and the experimental group, containing only individuals who will be exposed. Experimental studies are the strongest form of statistical study because the subjects are randomly divided into control and experimental groups prior to the introduction of the causal factor in the experimental group. This precaution goes a long way towards preventing the interference of some other causal agent—besides the one being tested for—interfering with the results.

In the second type, or _prospective study_, the sample population consists of an experimental group, which has already been exposed to the suspected cause, and a control group of individuals who have not been exposed. Then, as time passes, the experimenter observes whether any particular effects distinguish the two groups.

Suppose a study of the second type concerned the dropout rate at two high schools, call them "McKinley High School" and "Kepler High School." Which students go to which school has already been decided by district organizing, the location of the students' residences and other factors. To minimize other factors which may influence the outcome of the study, the experimenters focus on the freshmen students at the two schools. By graduation time, school records indicate that 28% of McKinley students have stopped attending classes (and have not transferred, died, etc.) while only 17% of Kepler students have (with all the relevant provisos). The experimenters, noting this dramatic difference, might try to draw some conclusions about the causal efficacy of initial differences between the two groups of freshmen, perhaps demographic, racial, or of some other type. Of course, prospective studies are naturally weaker than experimental ones simply because of the lack of control over which individuals fall into which of the two groups. In fact, there may be factors—unknown to the researchers—

which lie behind the distribution of individuals into McKinley or Kepler and which play a causal role in bringing about the observed effect. Perhaps there is a cultural difference prevailing at the two schools, due to the availability of good full-time employment available for teenagers in the vicinity of McKinley. An opportunity like this could well provide a strong temptation for McKinley students but not for ones at Kepler.

The final type of statistical study is retrospective. From the very meaning of "retrospective," one can immediately see that these studies are "backwards-looking." Say, for instance, some scientists are interested in the link between cigarette smoking and heart disease. Again, they start with two groups but, in a retrospective study, the groups consist of those who do and those who do not have the effect. In the present case, the effect would be heart disease. So the experiment would begin by selecting a group of heart disease victims and a group free from any cardiac troubles. Then the experimenters look backwards and compare the proportion, in each group, of those who did and those who did not smoke. Suppose that, in the heart disease group, 70% were smokers (and 30% non-smokers) and, in the group of those who did not develop heart disease, only 30% were smokers (and 70% were not). The experimenters would then conclude that there is a positive correlation between cigarette smoking and the later development of heart disease. But in retrospective studies, the evidence supports the conclusion very weakly, since there is virtually no way to control for other causal factors.

Suppose that, in another retrospective study, it was established that cigarette smoking is correlated with living in cities. This led critics of the first study to claim that it may well have been urban conditions—like pollution and the stress from living in high-density areas—which were the causes of the heart disease, not cigarette smoking. These criticisms nearly repudiated the retrospective studies of the relation between smoking and heart disease, which had already been completed. The only

when looking at an arguement, they probably wont say what type recourse the experimenters had was to repeat the experiment on a number of groups with different demographics. Finally, after many repetitions—which all showed a positive correlation between smoking and heart disease—the evidence became overwhelming.

In this case, as in most retrospective studies, there are serious considerations that prohibit the use of experimental studies and necessitate the use of weaker forms of statistical studies. Typically, the kinds of conditions in question exist when there is a suspicion that an agent is in any way harmful to human beings. In these cases, it would be immoral to conduct an experimental study in which the suspected cause is purposefully introduced to an experimental group. Although it is only through extensive repetition that retrospective studies can acquire compelling credibility, they have the advantage that oftentimes the necessary data are available and merely require analysis. For instance, entomologists wondering about the possible causes of colony collapse disorder among bees might study data from aviaries to learn about the effects of past viruses, temperature fluctuations, and other factors. This type of investigation, performed in the initial stages of the hunt for potential causes, provides a time- and money-saving method for finding a clue to guide more thorough investigation.

It is, however, possible to predict, in advance of any study, the numerical results that would be required to establish the kind of causal relation under investigation. Before proceeding to describe how these conclusions are obtained, it is first important to emphasize the need for large populations. If, for instance, a cause is under investigation that may affect all humans, any sample tested will be but a minute portion of the actual population. The failure to realize the significance of large populations in warranting conclusions is the source of many prejudices. For instance, one could imagine running into a person who was bigoted about Hoosits, the inhabitants of Hoositania, a nation of some 500 million. Our bigot might maintain that the problem with Hoosits, as he sees it, is that they are all lazy. When asked what his evidence for his "conclusion" might be, he answers, "Well, every Hoosit I've ever met was the laziest dirty dog you ever did see." But even if it is supposed that his statement is true, it does not make the least difference. The total number of Hoosits he's met—whether it's twenty, or forty, or a hundred—is too small a sample size to lend any significance to his conclusion.

Consider what happens when balls are drawn from an urn containing half blue and half red balls. If two balls are drawn, then the chances of drawing a ratio identical to the ratio of the general population of balls is exactly 50%. That is hardly better than the toss of a coin. But, without demonstrating it, what happens as more and more balls are drawn at the same time, the chances of drawing balls in the same exact proportion as the general population are less than half! The chances have actually decreased!

But this surprising—and apparently worrisome—result is balanced by the fact that the likelihood of drawing a sample with a proportion of red to blue balls, which is close to the actual ratio of the general population, has increased significantly. Indeed, if exactly 100 balls were drawn from the urn, 95% of all draws would fall in the range of 40 to 60 red balls and, if the draws were increased to 1000 balls, the percentage of draws between 480 and 520 red balls would be 95%.

If, however, the actual distribution in the total population were unknown, then the matter needs to be approached from the opposite direction. Suppose 1000 balls are drawn from the unknown population. If the draw results in exactly 500 red and 500 blue balls, then the likelihood that the distribution is between 470 and 530 balls of one color is 95%. In other words, out of a total of 20 draws, 19 would contain between 470 and 530 balls. The margin of error in this case is 30 balls, one way or another, out of the total of 1000 balls, or +/- 3%. In this basis, it is possible to generalize, concluding that, in samples of

1000 draws, the margin of error is 30/1000% or 3%. Margin of error depends entirely on sample size and, as explained earlier, decreases inversely with sample size. Here are a few margins of error for different sample sizes:

Sample Size and Margin of Error

25	+/- 22%
50	+/- 14%
100	+/- 10%
500	+/- 4%
1000	+/- 3%
1500	+/- 2%

(Interestingly, most political polls announced on television news shows indicate a margin of error of at least 3%, meaning that no more than 1000 citizens were polled.)

The relationships displayed in the table imply that the credibility of a statistical study depends directly on margin of error, which corresponds to sample size. This may be phrased in another way. Suppose, for example, that researchers investigate the relationship between pre-school exposure to reading and later success in school. They divide the sample population into preschoolers whose parents read to them at least three times a week and those who were not. Then they correlate these factors with later success in school, measured by grade average upon high school graduation. What they find is that 70% of the "read-to" preschoolers graduate with a B average or higher. Yet 70% of those who did not hear stories read as preschoolers graduated with less than a B average. What can be learned from the foregoing discussion (and the summary table above) is that it is impossible to determine the credibility of the study without more information.

This is a particularly important point to keep in mind when reading an account of a statistical study in the popular press. Unless the journalist provides the reader with a specification of the sample size or the margin of error, one simply cannot know what the study's worth or, in other words, its level of significance. In these terms, one can say that the level of significance of the conclusion that the actual result falls in the interval of the margin of error with a likelihood of 95% is at the .05 level. The figure of .05 is derived from the difference between the percentage of likelihood and complete certainty, or 100%.

****

The discussion of this chapter has focused on the inferential methods commonly employed by scientists and engineers to evaluate, assess, and test their ideas. To understand their methodology required the introduction of some specialized terminology so that the unconscious, implicit reasoning of technical professionals can be brought into the open, in order to be analyzed, appraised, and ultimately better understood. The purpose of these efforts is not to discover the flaws in their patterns of inference, but to follow their thinking when they come to judge the flashes of insight that come to them in those Eureka! Moments which are part of their professional careers. For the process of reasoning to which scientists and engineers subject their most brilliant glimpses into the nature of reality or how an artifact might work to bring about a desired result. And this stage in the process of scientific and technological development is crucial, for it provides the link between the original concepts and the ultimate touchstone of their worth – testing.

References

1. Oscar Handlin, "Science and Technology in Popular Culture," in G. Holton, ed. *A Study of Cohesive and Disjunctive Forces.* (Boston: Houghton Mifflin, 1965). P. 189.

2. R. N. Giere, John Bickle, and Robert Mauldin. *Understanding Scientific Reasoning.* (Belmont CA: Wadsworth Cengage Learning, 2006). Ch. 5.

3. Gottlob Frege, "Begriffschrifft," in Jean van Heijenoort, ed. *From Frege to Gödel.* (Cambridge, MA: Harvard University Press, 1967). Pp. 1-82; Bertrand Russell. *The Principles of Mathematics.* (London: George Allen and Unwin, 1903).

4. Stephen Jay Gould, "The Episodic Nature of Evolutionary Change," in *The Panda's Thumb.* (New York: W. W. Norton and Co., 1980), pp. 179-185.

4 Ways to Evaluate an arguement

1. Are the premises true?
2. Is the conclussion based on a logical analysis of the information given?
3. Is the conclussion relevant to the claim?
4. Are the claims and the conclussion staating the same information.

EXERCISES

Multiple-Choice

_____ 1. Justification, in both science and technology, consists of two components, _____ and _____.
  a. usefulness … moral good.
  b. data … prediction.
  c. hypothesis … experiment.
  d. logic … observation. ◄

_____ 2. _____ are regarded abstractly, as simply strings or sequences of statements.
  a. Antecedents
  b. Propositions
  c. Arguments ·
  d. Consequences

_____ 3. In a _____ argument, the premises purport to guarantee or compel the truth of the conclusion.
  a. consequential
  b. statistical
  c. inductive
  d. deductive.

_____ 4. In the argument:
      (i) All unmarried men are bachelors,
      (ii) Josh is an unmarried man,
      (iii) Josh is a bachelor,

   line (ii) is a _____, while line (iii) is a _____ of the argument
  a. premise … conclusion
  b. proposition … statement
  c. inference … solution
  d. observation … outcome

_____ 5. The _____ is the part of the conditional statement immediately following the "if," while the _____ follows the "then."
  a. antecedent ... consequent
  b. premise ... conclusion
  c. variable ... value
  d. possibility ... outcome

True/False

_____ 1. In a valid deductive argument, the truth of the premises guarantees the truth of the conclusion.

_____ 2. An argument is valid only when the truth of its premises and conclusions is certain.

_____ 3. To call a statement a conditional is to describe its form; it says nothing about its quantity, or the number of things to which it applies.

_____ 4. In an experimental study, the sample population includes an experimental group, which has already been exposed to the suspected cause, and a control group of individuals, who have not been exposed.

_____ 5. The margin of error does not depend on the sample size.

_____ 6. The argument
  (i) All unmarried men are bachelors,
  (ii) Josh is an unmarried man,
  (iii) Josh is a bachelor,
  is a valid deductive argument in standard form.

_____ 7. To determine the level of significance, one must know the sample size and/or the margin of error.

_____ 8. If P and Q are independent, it is impossible to accept both P and Q.

_____ 9. The recognition of the independence of evolution and the rate of speciation was key to the development of a new model of evolutionary change.

_____ 10. A sound argument is a valid argument that has true premises.

Discussion Questions

1.   This chapter discusses three (3) types of statistical arguments: experimental studies, prospective studies, and retrospective studies. Make up an example study for each type. For each example, make sure you fully consider and explain all the possible shortcomings of that type of study.

2.   Create a list of criteria that you could use to evaluate any or all of the types of arguments discussed in this chapter.

3.   As citizens, we are continually confronted with information about our health: what we should eat and what we shouldn't, what medicines we should take and which medicines we shouldn't, what products we should use and what we shouldn't. Think of behavior you've changed because you've heard or read that something is or isn't healthy. Re-analyze the arguments that forced you to change your behavior. Why did you trust them in the first place? To be on the "safe side," should you continue to trust them? Should you tell your friends to change their behavior as well? Should you wait for further studies that confirm the conclusions?

4

TESTING

Go, wondrous creature! Mount where
Sciences guides; Go, measure earth,
weigh air, and state the tides;
Instruct the planets in what orbs to run,
Correct old Time, and regulate the sun...

-Alexander Pope, *"An Essay on Man"*

The standards of inference discussed in the previous chapter are key to understanding the thinking of specialists in science and technology as well as to set standards for any inquiry into their relation to society. But it is important to keep in mind that reasoning is simply a means to an end, the means used to relate beliefs to their justification. In science and technology both, the ultimate touchstone of truth is observation, a point that is emphasized when it is said that science and technology are empirical endeavors. Since, of course, observation tends to be highly subjective, colored by the observer's moods, desires, and perhaps even their last meal, science has, over the centuries, introduced limits and boundaries to render observation uniform from observer to observer. In the final analysis, the import and merit carried by an individual's observation is enhanced and amplified by its agreement with the observations of other qualified observers. Strictly speaking, it is the consensus of qualified observers which is the real touchstone of truth in scientific and technical fields. Naturally, even the most broadly accepted observation may, upon further investigation, turn out to be mistaken, so all observational evidence—without exception—is corrigible and may be revised in the light of further experience.

The focus of the present chapter is directed towards the process of deriving particular statements from generalizations in order to grasp the power of an hypothesis to explain phenomena or to test the accuracy of an hypothesis against observation. Of course, most people are well aware that observation is the touchstone of scientific truth. They know, in other words, that hypotheses are not accepted by scientists without reason and that the most convincing reason of all -in science- is observation. What few people do not seem to grasp are the inferential relations between the statements which are actually compared to observations or experimental outcomes and the hypotheses which are tested by them. This is surprising, because these relations are actually quite simple. But the simplicity of the basic relations is complicated by the fact that the heuristic force of an observational or experimental outcome is profoundly influenced by the context. The examples in this chapter range from medical experiments where human life was at stake to astronomical observations which were unconcerned with life or death issues, but which shaped our understanding of our place -as human beings- in the cosmos. On one understanding, astronomy placed the earth at the center of the universe, reinforcing the religious belief that mankind was the supreme achievement of the Creator. On the other, the planet occupied by mankind was moved to third position from the sun, thus demoting mankind to a secondary or tertiary status. Obviously, the stakes in these cases were not at all the same. Consequently, people tend to think the scientific process involved, especially the relations of observations to hypotheses, were not at all the same. But the argument of this chapter shows that, for the most part, the inferential reasoning in all these cases is quite uniform. And what that means for the development of a critical understanding of scientific reasoning is that, once the application of the common inferential patterns common to thinking about science or technology are grasped, it is a simple matter to analyze any similar situation.

Explanation and Prediction

The discussion of the last chapter focused on the relations of the general and the particular. In some cases, the object is to show that a universal generalization "covers" (or applies to) a particular case and, in that sense, explains it. For instance, one might apply the laws of motion to show that a particular falling object—say the mythical apple that hit Newton in the head—fell just as the laws say it should. When a particular event occurs before it is related to a universal generalization, the process of covering it with a generalization is called "explaining" the event. In contrast, when the particular event is to occur in the future, its derivation from a universal statement is called a "prediction." The difference between explanations and predictions is just a matter of when the inferential relation is established relative to the time the particular event occurs.

Newton and the Apple

The logical schema of the procedure for explanation and prediction—or for testing generally—involves a hypothesis, call it "H," and an observation, call it "O," related to the hypothesis. The first thing to notice is that the inference

H

O

cannot possibly be valid. The reason is that, since H is a hypothesis, it has the form of a universal conditional, i.e.

H: For all x, if x is F, then x is G,

or, in other words

All F's are G's,

which simply says that all objects possessing the property F also possess the property G. To infer anything from H, it is first necessary to specify a particular individual, call it "a," which has the property F or,

Fa.

Invoking Fa as an additional premise, that is,

For all x, if x is F, then x is G
Fa

Ga,

results in a valid argument.[1]

This inferential pattern provides the basic model for the reasoning of scientists and engineers in the testing of their ideas, whether those ideas are scientific theories about the natural world or conceptions of devices or artifacts to achieve certain pragmatic ends. This pattern of reasoning has come to be called the "Hypothetico-Deductive (or just H-D) Model" and

F is a property of the sample, X

it has proved extremely successful in schematizing the complex reasoning involved in the creation of science and technology.

To explain the H-D model, the philosopher Carl Hempel told a charming story about the efforts of the Viennese physician, Ignasz Semmelweis, to reduce the incidence of puerpheral—more commonly called "child-bed"—fever in the First Clinic of Vienna General Hospital in the early 19th Century. It struck Semmelweis as somewhat curious that the mortality rate from the fever in the First Clinic was much higher than it was in the hospital's other ward, the Second Clinic. At the time, there was no well-articulated germ theory of disease, and no one—neither medical professionals nor laypeople—really believed that tiny organisms, invisible to the naked eye, played any role in the propagation of disease. This may be somewhat hard to believe, given that nearly two centuries earlier the father of microbiology, Antonie von Leeuwenhoek, had observed "animalcules" with one of his instruments. But it was only after repeated efforts

Antonie van Leeuwenhoek

that Semmelweis identified a cause of the high rate of infection and took steps to curtail it. What's most telling about the story of Semmelweis' efforts is that it illustrates how common-sense trial-and-error methods become, with a little refinement and some organization, the principal means used by scientists and engineers to discover and verify their hypotheses. In other words, one should take the story of Semmelweis as evidence that science is a carefully organized and regimented version of common sense processes. Semmelweis repeatedly tried out his ideas about the origins of child-bed fever by simply eliminating the suspected cause and observing the result. One could just as well describe his work as the repeated proposal of hypotheses about the sources of the malady, the derivation of predictions from these hypotheses, and the observation of outcomes.

One idea Semmelweis tried out was concerned the birth position of the mother. He developed this hypothesis by reflecting on the fact that, in the Second Clinic where the incidence of child-bed fever was lower, mid-wives delivered the babies from mothers lying on their sides, rather than the usual supine position. Semmelweis reasoned that, if the <u>mother's position during childbirth was the cause</u>, it could be tested by positioning the women on their sides during birth, rather than the usual supine position. Unfortunately, when the women in the First Clinic started delivering their babies on their sides, the mortality rate remained unchanged.

Ignasz Semmelweis

Another idea was that women in the First Clinic tended to arrive at the hospital at the last minute, some even giving birth before their arrival. But when he studied the group who had experienced so-called "street births" more closely, Semmelweis found that their mortality rate was actually much lower than the rest of the population of the First Clinic. Perhaps the most curious of Semmelweis' hypotheses concerned the administration of the <u>Last Sacraments to women</u> in the Clinic dying of the disease. The administration of the sacrament was accompanied by a mini-procession of an altar boy ringing a bell and a priest carrying the sacrament. Semmelweis reasoned that witnessing this spectacle had a negative psychological effect on the other women in the ward, causing despondency which undermined their health. To test this hypothesis, Semmelweis instructed the priest to abandon the procession through the Clinic in favor of a less prominent route to the needy patient. In addition, Semmelweis ordered a stop to the bell-ringing. Alas, there was still no improvement.

The tragic twist of fate which guided Semmelweis to his

crucial discovery came when a colleague was accidentally cut by a scalpel wielded by a medical student. The student had been dissecting a corpse in anatomy class when he slipped and cut his professor. Within days, Semmelweis' colleague developed symptoms remarkably similar to those of the new mothers suffering from child-bed fever. Semmelweis figured that the same material transferred by the scalpel to his associate was also being transferred to the pregnant mothers in the maternity ward. As fate would have it, the women were routinely examined by medical students following their anatomy class, in which they regularly dissected human corpses. Thus Semmelweis formulated the hypothesis:

> H: Material from the cadavers is being transferred to the pregnant women by the medical students.

Like his previous tests, Semmelweis attempted to interrupt the action of the cause. This was done, simply enough, by requiring the medical students to wash their hands in strong soap between their anatomy class and their examination of the expectant women. Lo and behold! The mortality rate in the ward dropped to astonishing levels!

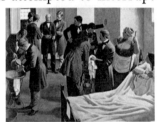

Semmelweis and Medical Students

The Hypothetico-Deductive Model

The usefulness of the H D model is illustrated by it use as a tool in the analysis of Semmelweis' efforts. Strictly speaking, the H-D model is just a scheme for a simple deductive argument with a universal conditional (or hypothetical) statement as its principal premise. The second premise is just the instantiation

of the first part of the conditional (the "antecedent"), and
the conclusion is just the instantiation of the final part of the
conditional premise (or the "consequent"). Thus,

> 1.   For all x, if x is F, then x is G, (Hypothesis)
> 2.   a is an F, (From antecedent of (1))
>
> ———————————————————————
>
> 3.   a is a G. (From consequent of (1)).

Of course, the H-D model is a valid deductive argument
form. Any instantiation of the H-D model in which (1) and
(2) are true will also have a true conclusion of the form (3). If
the H-D model is used to represent the testing of a scientific
hypothesis, then (1) represents the hypothesis, or the principal
contention being tested. (2) would then be a statement of
the initial conditions of the test, the situation created in the
laboratory or observed in nature in which the principal factor
under scrutiny, the property F, has been introduced to the
sample, represented by "a."

This much fine detail is hardly necessary to capture the
structure of the argument implicit in these episodes of scientific
reasoning. For instance, we might just let "H" stand for whatever
hypothesis is under discussion, ignoring momentarily the finer
details of the generality or conditional structure of the argument.
Then, each of Semmelweis' hypotheses can be represented by
the letter "H," subscripted to indicate the various hypotheses.
Thus

> H1= the fever was caused by birth position,
> H2 = the fever was caused by delays in arrival at
>   the hospital,
> H3 = the fever was caused by the despondent
>   moods of the mothers due to witnessing the
>   administration of the Last Sacrament,

and so on. Of course, the remaining premises will also be altered to reflect the difference in hypotheses. But the conclusion, indicating a decline in the incidences of child-bed fever in the ward, will be the same.

But there are complications. For instance, suppose the H-D Model were used to describe one of the observations of the moons of Jupiter reported by Galileo in The Starry Messenger (1610). In this case, the first premise might have been a claim about the appearance of one of the moons on one side of Jupiter so many days after its disappearance (behind Jupiter) on the other side. The first premise might be something like

> 4. Whenever a telescope is aimed to observe the left side of Jupiter four days after the disappearance of one of its moons on the right side, the missing moon will be observed to re-appear.

And the next premise would have the form of

> 5. On the 23rd of November, 1609, a telescope was positioned to observe the left side of Jupiter.

And the conclusion would be something like:

> 6. On the 23rd of November, 1609, a moon was observed to appear on the left side of Jupiter.

Less detail is usually sufficient to capture the broad pattern of a scientist's or engineer's reasoning. Instead of the carefully detailed representation just sketched, one might just let "H" stand for the principal hypothesis under scrutiny, "IC" represent the initial conditions of the test, and "P" stand for the prediction to be observed. Then the H-D Model has the simple schematic pattern

H
IC

———

P.

Of course, it must be understood that the schema represents a valid deductive argument.

Still, some critics might object that this schema is just a little too simple, for it leaves out crucial details. For instance, there

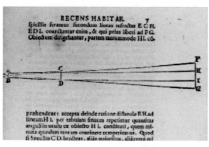

Galileo's Optical Theory

are almost always other claims, besides the principal hypothesis under test, which are required in order to validly draw the conclusion from the principal hypothesis and initial conditions. Such an "auxiliary hypothesis" might concern the workings of any instruments involved in the test, like the spyglass which Galileo used to observe the moons of Jupiter. At the time, there was no fully articulated optical theory to explain the workings of Galileo's spyglass in the kind of detail common today, but he had a good idea of how its configuration of lenses worked. The usual account is that one of his students, who had been touring the Low Countries, reported that he had seen spyglasses used as novelties on the streets of Amsterdam. Galileo immediately figured out the lenses needed to observe celestial bodies, ordered a pair with the properties he thought optimal, and the rest is history. So he did have some idea of how the spyglass worked and this idea should be represented as an element in the argument.

An interesting historical detail turns on Galileo's "theory" of optics. The prevailing cosmology at the time was derived from Aristotle, considered a scientific authority by the Church.

Aristotle maintained that the domain below the orbit of the moon was wholly unlike the domain of the moon and celestial objects beyond it. For one thing, objects below the lunar orbit were subject to decay and corruption. Their motion was rectilinear, either to or from the earth, while the motion of all celestial objects

Galileo and his Spyglass

was circular. So when Galileo first displayed his spyglass to Church authorities, they granted its fidelity for terrestrial matters, but questioned its ability to represent celestial objects faithfully. Obviously, it was a key presumption of Galileo's thoughts on optics that Aristotle's division of the cosmos into terrestrial and celestial spheres was invalid. Hence, if t he telescope represented earthly objects faithfully, its images of heavenly ones were also faithful to the original.

Let "AH" represent Galileo's auxiliary hypothesis about the workings of the spyglass. Then the H-D model becomes

H
IC & AH
_____

P

When the derived prediction is actually observed, then all the elements of the premises—including the principal hypothesis, the description of the initial conditions, as well as the auxiliary hypothesis used in the deduction—are confirmed. Since, of course, the confirmed premises are contingent statements, the confirmation they receive is only partial and tentative. A future test, in which things do not come out as predicted, would undermine whatever credibility they might have gained from a successful test. And how much their credibility is increased by a particular successful test is a matter of degree, to be decided by experts on the basis of such considerations as how dramatic or unusual the prediction (given the background knowledge, and other similar factors).

Falsification

But this raises an important point: if the prediction turns out well, then the degree to which an hypothesis is warranted is increased, but it is still a matter of degree. In particular, the hypothesis is not completely and fully verified ("once and for all time," so to speak). On the other hand, consider what happens when a prediction like Galileo's ("P," in the schema above) fails. What is usually thought is that the failure of a prediction conclusively falsifies the hypothesis in question. Such a view is sometimes called "naïve falsificationism" because it overlooks the ambiguity inherent in cases of the failure of predictions.

Cases of predictive failures are handled by trotting out the H-D model for the case

H
IC & AH
_____

P

and determining the effect the prediction's failure, or Not-P. It is important, first of all, to observe that the entire argument of the model may be cast in the form of a conditional, thus:

If (H & IC & AH), then P.

Then the question is what can be concluded from the conditional form and the actual predictive failure. In other words, what conclusion could be validly drawn from the premises

> If (H & IC & AH), then P,
> Not-P?

First of all, the following argument

> If (H & IC & AH), then P,
> Not-P
> ———————————————
> Not-H

is invalid. So the failure of a prediction does not imply that the hypothesis being tested is false. What the failure of the premise shows is that one of the original premises—H or IC or AH—is false. In other words, the argument

> If (H & IC & AH), then P,
> Not-P?
> ———————————————
> not-H or not-IC or not-AH

is valid. But that is just to say that, in the cases of a failed prediction, one cannot validly infer that the principal hypothesis in question is false. Rather, one can only infer that the principal hypothesis or the description of the initial conditions or an auxiliary hypothesis is false. Thus a failed prediction alone is insufficient grounds for rejecting the main hypothesis under scrutiny. This is just to say the failure of a prediction establishes that (at least) one of the premises is false, but does not specify which one. It could be any one of H, IC, and AH. (This fact could be called "the fickle finger of falsification"!)

Of course, we can never be certain which of the possible culprits is the false one. This has led some thinkers to claim that all of the premises are equally likely to be the source of the failure. So one can never have any reason to decide which it is. Consequently, cases of predictive failure always involve a conventional moment in which the decision to hold one, rather than another of the premises responsible is an arbitrary decision. This position is sometimes called "naïve falsificationism."

Nonetheless, in practice, this situation is unlikely to arise. For one thing, the likelihood that the statement of initial conditions—"IC" in the schema—is true is increased by the presence of several observers independently ascertaining the experimental or observational set-up. And since auxiliary hypotheses usually concern the workings of the scientific instruments employed, the possibility of a false auxiliary hypothesis can be minimized through the use of tried and tested instruments. Still, errors can arise, which just emphasizes the idea that no statement in science is infallible.

Crucial Experiments

In certain situations, two different hypotheses or theories will compete to explain the same domain of phenomena. Such a situation typically involves an established theory for a given domain and a newly conceived challenger. This may occur when the domains of the hypotheses or theories exactly coincide or, on the other hand, their respective domains may just overlap on a common area. When competition between alternative hypotheses arises, scientists strive to design an experiment which will confirm one of the hypotheses or theories while disconfirming the other. Such an experiment would provide a dramatic test, more conclusively demonstrating the superiority of one of the proposed explanatory frameworks, than an ordinary test of a single hypothesis in isolation could. An experiment of this sort is called a "crucial experiment" because of its decisive ability to select between two hypotheses or theories.

Galileo and the Phases of Venus

An example of this type of experiment arose at the very beginning of the Scientific Revolution, when Copernicus

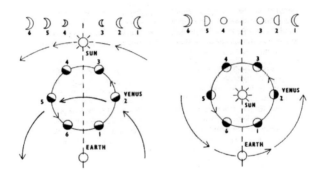

Ptolemaic and Copernican Views of Venus

reasoned that, if his heliocentric hypothesis was right, and the planets really did orbit the sun, then Venus should exhibit a full range phases, just like the moon (new moon, full moon, etc.). Copernicus thought the phases of Venus would provide a decisive refutation of the Ptolemy's geocentric world-view and his own sun-centered conception.[2] Yet the phases had never been observed, a fact which dismayed Copernicus.[3] But shortly after Galileo turned his telescope to the night-sky, he received a letter from his student

Benedetto Castelli, asking whether Galileo had observed the phases of Venus with his telescope.[4] Apparently, Galileo had observed changes in Venus' appearance, but he had failed to observe Venus systematically. Consequently, he had not observed the full range of phases predicted by Copernicus' theory. It was not long, however, before he fully verified Coperncius' prediction. And he began to report to Castelli –in coded language- that Venus goes through phases like the moon. It was not long, however, before he did fully verify this. The detection of the phases of Venus was a dramatic confirmation of Copernicus' heliocentric hypothesis, since it showed that Venus was illuminated by the light of the sun as it orbited around it. At the same time, the observation of Venus' phases disproved the prevailing geocentric astronomy of Ptolemy. According the Ptolemaic hypothesis, Venus would either be behind the sun and fully illuminated, or between the earth and the sun – which would make it appear completely dark. Basically, Venus would appear either fully illuminated or fully darkened, with no intermediate stages between the extremes. Galileo's observations established Venus goes through a range of stages between the extremes. The implication is that Venus must revolve around the sun, as the Copernican hypothesis predicted, and not, as Ptolemy

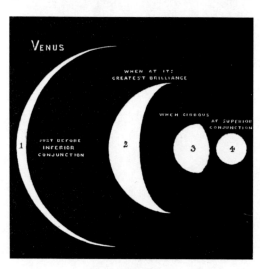

Phases of Venus

thought, around the earth.

The relation between the different hypotheses and Galileo's observations can be represented as two different H-D schemas, one for each of the hypotheses. First, the various components in the schemas must be identified.

H1   Copernican Heliocentric Theory
H2   Ptolemaic Geocentric Theory
IC   Details of the focus and aim of Galileo's telescope, the weather conditions, time of day (or night), etc. on the various occasions of observation.
AH   Optical Theory of the Telescope
O   Galileo's observations of the phases of Venus.

Then there are two schemas representing the inferential relations of the two hypotheses to Galileo's observations. The schema on the left shows Copernicus' prediction of the phases of Venus and the second the Ptolemaic prediction:

H1	H2
IC	IC
AH	AH
———	———
O	not-O

Since the Copernican hypothesis (H1) predicts what was actually observed (O), the observation confirms the hypothesis, just as the schema shows. According to the second schema, however, the Ptolemaic hypothesis (H2) predicts that Galileo would not observe the phases (not-O). But, in fact, he did. So H2 must be false. And this example displays the power of crucial experiments to decide between competing hypotheses.

The Shape of the Earth

The debate goes back to Christian Huyghens and Isaac Newton, both of whom believed the earth was flattened at the poles (or oblate) even though they were working with different theories of gravitation. But their hypotheses were based on rather flimsy evidence: pendulum data compiled near the

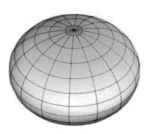

Prolate Spheroid   **Oblate Spheroid**

equator, which showed that gravity was less there than at higher latitudes. But a new set of relevant data emerged from a major effort to map the kingdom of France, including measurements of celestial arcs and terrestrial distances. Jacques Cassini deduced from these data that the earth was elongated (or prolate) rather than oblate. His hypothesis was not challenged until 1730, when a group of mathematicians from the Paris Academy doubted the accuracy of the sort of local measurements Cassini had used. So the Royal Treasury funded two expeditions, one to the equator and one to Lapland, to collect data which could be compared to resolve the issue. The significance of the issue derives from the factions involved. In favor of a prolate earth were the Cartesians, followers of Rene Descartes who is primarily remembered today for Cartesian geometry and the foundational statement of his philosophical system ("I think, therefore I am"). In his System of the World, Descartes had hypothesized that the planets were carried about in huge vortices, which whirled them about in their orbits and simultaneously spun them in their daily revolutions. Thus the planets should be prolate. Descartes' ideas were very popular in France, not only because he was himself French but also because he had published his ideas nearly a century earlier. But Pierre Louis Maupertuis, along with the mathematicians of the Paris Academy, was a proponent of the system of physics constructed by Isaac Newton in his Principia of 1687. Newton's work was barely known in France but was energetically promoted by a select few supporters. Thus the issue came down to the Cartesians, who favored a prolate earth, versus the Newtonians who believed that the earth must be oblate. In 1738, Maupertuis set off with an expedition to Lapland and another expedition set out to make their measurements near the equator. When they reported back to Paris, the conclusion was unambiguous: the earth was oblate, just as Newton had predicted.[1]

Observational Evidence

But this discussion of how evidence is related to hypotheses is incomplete without some mention of how claims about evidence are accepted. The question, in other words, concerns how a prediction is confirmed or falsified by actual observation. Since one of the hallmarks of modern science and technology is their dependence on observation, it is important to see how observation is actually related to the inferential chains tying technical claims to one another. After all, the acceptance of claims in science and technology depends not only on their connections to observational claims, but how those claims come to be accepted or rejected by the relevant community of professionals. In this connection, it is useful to consider the regimentation and control of observation which emerged in the early days of the Scientific Revolution.

In *Leviathan and the Air-Pump*, the authors describe how, in its early days, the Royal Society required that its experiments would be conducted publicly, so qualified observers could observe the trial together at the same time. This method recognizes that observations of experimental results must be intersubjective, or available to a number of observers. Then, for instance, an event that could, in principle, be witnessed by only one observer—like a dream or certain types of UFO sightings—would be excluded from consideration. Somebody who considered a dream as evidence of a physical event would be relying on a standard of acceptable evidence far lower than that of the early Royal Society. Indeed, the standards of groups like the Society are the result of discussion and deliberation, ultimately resting on a consensus prevailing among the members of the Society.

In addition, the Royal Society required that the witnesses of experiments whose judgments contributed to the consensus should also meet certain conditions. First of all, they must be gentlemen of leisure, undistracted by other pursuits or, in other words, they must be disinterested observers, who stood neither to gain nor lose financially from the outcome of an experiment. At the same time the Royal Society was establishing these conditions, Robert Boyle was writing descriptions of the experiments which would provide a more lasting contribution to the literature. For Boyle attempted to write up experimental procedures in such a way that anyone who read his reports would "virtually experience" whatever any observer on the scene would have observed. In other words, he focused on those circumstances of the experiment which would be essential ingredients of any re-enactment, thus specifying

Robert Boyle

exactly what one had to do in order to duplicate the efforts of the experimenter. Although it seems likely that Boyle's intent was to convince the reader that the experimental set-up produced the outcome reported, he accomplished this by demonstrating the features of the experiment which made it replicable by any competent experimenter. His efforts served as a first step towards identifying a key feature of any minimally satisfactory experiment: it must be replicable.

Some of the most famous experiments in the history of science were attempts to replicate a procedure which had been previously performed by another experimenter. Typically, experiments are not repeated unless there is reason to doubt the outcome. In recent years, however, there has been significant controversy concerning experiments to produce cold fusion based on the inability of well-qualified experimenters to reproduce the original experiments. Strictly speaking, the failure of a research team to obtain the same experimental results from the same set-up does not invalidate the work of another team. But it does undermine the credibility of their work, depending on the competence of the other team.

More often, replications are not true to the original, but simulate another experiment with a minor variation in one particular respect that the experimenter thinks might prove significant. In a case like this, an investigator might study the experiment of another group and wonder what might happen if some detail of the set-up were changed. Then, of course, she tries it for herself – sometimes with surprising results.

Of course, the efforts of every investigator, aimed at eliminating the possibility that causes, other than those under investigation, have acted on the experimental set-up to bring about its result. That is to say, the experimenter must control all other variables than the ones being studied, thus eliminating any variation which might interfere with the outcome. Thus, what counts as evidence in science and technology consists of sources which are controlled. A controlled experiment or observation is one in which possible causes of the effect under investigation, besides the cause studied, are not allowed to vary. This is easiest to bring about in a laboratory setting or other environment that re-creates natural conditions as closely as possible while isolating them from interference from any sources other than those under investigation. For instance, supernatural visions, no matter how intimately related to matters which have been worrying a person, might really be brought about by a plunge in one's blood-sugar level, rather than the intervention of other-worldly forces. It is precisely causes of this sort, which may be prevented by controlling the conditions of the vision, in order to see if it arises when blood-sugar levels are normal. Remember how Scrooge dismissed Marley's ghost in Charles Dickens' classic, A Christmas Carol? Scrooge said that the apparition might be nothing more than a bit of undigested cheese. And that is

Scrooge and Marley

just to say that there were other, equally plausible causes which might have caused Marley's appearance than the somewhat fantastic hypothesis that what Scrooge saw was, indeed, a ghost.

References

1.   Technically, the instantiation to the individual named by 'a' would have to occur before the second premise is introduced, so that the proper form of the argument would be

> For all x, if x is an F, then x is a G,
> If a is an F, then a is a G,
> a is an F_____
> Therefore, a is a G.

2.   Carl Hempel. *Philosophy of Natural Science.* (Englewood Cliffs, N.J.: Prentice-Hall, 966). Ch. 2.

3.   Nicolaus Copernicus. *On the Revolutions of the Heavenly Spheres.* i, 10. Later, Galileo lionized Copernicus for defending his commitment to the heliocentric hypothesis, despite the fact that the implication of the phases of Venus was contradicted by sensory evidence – unaided by the telescope.

4.   Quoted in Galileo Galilei. *Siderius Nuncius or The Sidereal Messenger.* Albert van Helden, trans. and ed. (Chicago: The University of Chicago Press, 1989). P. 106.

5.   Simon Shaffer and Steven Shapin. *Leviathan and the Air-Pump.* (Princeton: Princeton U. Pr., 1985). Ch. 2.

6.   Mary Terrall, *Representing the Earth's Shape: The Polemics Surrounding Maupertuis' Expedition to Lapland,* ISIS 1992, 83: 218-237.

EXERCISES

Multiple-Choice

_____ 1. The ultimate touchstone of truth in both science and technology is _____.
   a. observation.
   b. reason.
   c. marketability.
   d. repeatability.

_____ 2. Observations, reflecting the people making them, are subject to error. All observed evidence is corrigible and may be _____ in light of new _____.
   a. enhanced ... market focus.
   b. revised ... experience.
   c. directed ... project goals.
   d. ignored ... developments.

_____ 3. The Royal Society set standards for those taking scientific observations, suggesting that they must be gentlemen of leisure, _____ or, in other words, _____ observers, who stood to neither gain nor lose from the outcome of an experiment.
   a. involved in other industries ... devout
   b. who were lazy ... open-minded
   c. distracted by politics ... hardened
   d. undistracted by other pursuits.... disinterested

_____ 4. Robert Boyle's detailed accounts of experiments helped to establish a key criteria for any experiment: it must be _____.
   a. intuitive.
   b. simple.
   c. replicable.
   d. sterile.

_____ 5. (1) For all x, if x is F, then x is G

(2) Fa

_____

(3) Ga

"Fa" in the argument form above represents the experimental setup where "F" is a _____ and "a" is a _____.

   a. property ... sample.
   b. sample ... technique.
   c. observation ... outcome.
   d. premise ... conclusion.

True/False

_____ 1. Semmelweis knew about Germ Theory; that's why he made medical students wash their hands before delivering babies.

_____ 2. Galileo made observations about the moons of Mars.

_____ 3. Aristotle maintained that the domain below the orbit of the moon was wholly unlike the domain of the moon and celestial objects beyond it; that is why the church authorities doubted Galileo's telescope.

_____ 4. Copernicus reasoned that if the universe was heliocentric and Venus orbited the sun, Venus would have phases similar to the phases of the moon.

_____ 5. An observer's emotional responses to a prediction are equally important as observations in the decision to accept a theory.

Questions 6-10 refer to the following argument:

(1) For all x, if x is F, then x is G,

(2) a is an F,

_____

(3) a is a G.

_____ 6. If the argument above describes a particular experiment conforming to the H-D Model, then (1) is the hypothesis of the experiment.

_____ 7. Line (2) could be rephrased "F is a sample with the property a."

_____ 8. Line (2) represents the initial conditions of the experiment.

_____ 9. It is sometimes necessary to include "auxiliary hypotheses" (AH) in experimental arguments. These would contain further statements about the workings of the experimental design or any equipment use.

_____ 10. If (3) is found to be false, then suggesting that (1) or (2) is false is an example of "naïve falsificationism."

Discussion Questions

1.   To confirm you understand the H-D Model, make up your own example of an argument that fulfills the form. Remember to clearly define "x," "F," "G," and "a." Your example can be as simple or as complex as you'd like. (i.e., food you like, your favorite possessions, etc.)

2.   What do you think is the most interesting scientific discovery of the 18th-, 19th-, or 20th- centuries? What do you know about experiments that may have led to this discovery? Describe the experiment in terms of trial-and-error and of the H-D Model.

5

DYNAMICS

These portals, these columns prove
That skill, industry, art reside here;
Where action rules and idleness is banished
Vice cannot easily gain control.
I will boldly pass through that portal;
Its design is noble, straightforward, pure....

-Wolfgang Amadeus Mozart

In addition to the similarities and differences which contribute to the understanding of science and technology, it is also important to carefully consider how they respectively develop over time. First of all, there are important differences in the workaday life of scientists and engineers. Typically, a scientist outlines her aims and methodology in proposals to acquire funding but, once her grant or fellowship is awarded, she has considerable latitude to pursue the work promised, as long as she stays within the broad outlines sketched in her original proposal. Thus, scientists are less subject to direct control by their sponsors and are primarily responsible to the internal demands of science. Once the term of the award or grant expires, the scientist must file a formal report indicating results obtained under the award, with indications of future directions for further research. Again, the final report is a summary of work rather than a detailed, blow-by-blow account of the day-to-day progress of the research. Thus the scientist remains relatively free, within loosely defined bounds, to pursue her research.

Engineers developing new technologies are expected to produce practical outcomes which address particular stated problems. Unlike scientists, engineers are not afforded the opportunity to pursue new lines of inquiry that develop in the course of their work. Rather, they are expected to produce solutions within a limited scope of possibilities, which must succeed under quite rigorous conditions. Typically, engineers work in close proximity with senior engineers or managers charged with their supervision, reporting on the progress of their work far more frequently than scientists.

Incremental Improvement

One important respect in which science and technology differ considerably is in the dynamics of their development. Technology develops incrementally, through the accumulation of changes in an original innovation.

A classic example of the development of a technology through incremental improvements over time is provided by photography. Photography developed from the camera obscura, which was already known to Aristotle and was often used by painters and artists in the Renaissance, including Leonardo da Vinci. It consisted of a pinhole in the wall of a darkened room which allowed light to enter and projected an inverted image on the wall opposite the pinhole. By putting a pinhole in a wooden box with a transparent or translucent screen for one of its sides, scientists created a device for the safe observation of solar eclipses. In the early 19th Century, the pinhole was replaced by an optical lens which vastly improved the projected image. Chemical emulsions, developed in the 1820's and 1830's, allowed the preservation of images on paper. But photography did not flourish until the rise of the middle class in the latter part of the 19th Century. The burgeoning class of shopkeepers, craftsmen, and entrepreneurs desired portraits of themselves in rich surroundings to imitate the wealthy, who prized painted portraits of themselves. Portrait-artists were extremely busy and far too expensive for the rising middle-class. One of the first efforts to imitate the aristocratic, was the hand-coloured Daguerreotype in a leather case, which was an inexpensive imitation of the miniature portrait of aristocratic fashion. For some time, photographic portraits continued to resemble

Tintype

their bourgeois origins, thereby maintaining their function as a status symbol by duplicating traditional background of portraits, including carpets and drapes, armchairs and pedestal tables, rustic balustrades as well as numerous lush houseplants. The settings of the photos thus imitated the painted state portraits of the well-to-do. The dress and pose of the subjects completed the image of people conscious of their dignity.

Eventually, the desire for photographs spread throughout the population, with everyone wanting images of themselves for keepsakes, and for sharing with family or friends. This development provided an opening for a young entrepreneur who supplied light-sensitive glass plates to photographers, named George Eastman. In his drive to make photography as readily accessible as a common pencil, Eastman developed a method of applying the emulsions to paper. Surprisingly, the photographers who used glass-plates were uninterested in trying the film, which was much easier to use. So Eastman instead tried appealing to the general public in the late 1880's by marketing an "aim and shoot" camera which was the predecessor of the famous Kodak Brownie. His early cameras came with enough film for 100 photos. When they had been exposed, the customer simply shipped the camera back to Kodak. The camera was filled

George Eastman

with fresh film, the old film was developed, and the whole kit and caboodle was returned to the customer. All the customer had to do was "aim and shoot"— Kodak did the rest.

In 1900, Eastman had another idea and introduced the Kodak Brownie. The Brownie was so simple to use that it was marketed to school-age children and was sold for just $1.

Eastman's case illustrates the principle that successful innovation depends largely on the developer's perceptions of consumer wants and needs. It also shows that there is no point in developing and supplying a technology unless effective demand—the desire for the product and the ability to pay for it—already exists among its intended audience. The more radical an improvement, the more difficult it is to foresee its effect on the demand for a technology. There is an oft-repeated story about how an electronics manufacturer, Sony, asked marketing surveyors to determine whether consumers would purchase a small, portable tape recorder which did not even record, but only played back pre-recorded tapes. What the marketing specialists found was that the proposed product would be an abysmal failure, since consumers regarded it as generally useless. Sony disregarded the results and produced The Walkman, which sold 30,000 in the first two months after its introduction and 50 million within a decade! The moral of the story is not, however, that the marketing surveyors erred but that people may not be competent predictors of their own tastes and preferences.

Long-Term Development

Incremental development is obvious in any technology that has persisted for any length of time. Consider railroads, which have seen a gradual increase in freight capacity occur simultaneously with increases in motive power. Or the internal combustion engine which, when first introduced, suffered from a lack of power until the discovery of advanced ignition timing and the development of gasoline anti-knock additives, among

Tin Lizzie

other improvements. Meanwhile, early internal combustion engines clanked, sputtered, and barely ran, awaiting innovations that would quiet them down and make them run well. These improvements come from a wide range of sources—in the case of the internal combustion engine, advancements were suggested by professionals as diverse as engineers and auto mechanics. Great successes in the improvement of a technology seldom result from flashes of brilliance; more often than not, they are the result of a clever hunch about what might work,

Penicillin Surface Fermentation Vessel, c. 1942

gradually improved upon. Of course, when inventions are first introduced, they must establish demand or satisfy a pre-existing demand, before entering a shakedown period—typically quite protracted—during which they are continually improved and enhanced.

One of the most important stages in the development of a technology occurs during the product development stage, which transforms a workable innovation into a competitively priced invention, produced in sufficient quantities to take advantage of economies of scale. Although basic research is a time-consuming, expensive process, it seldom results in products ready for the marketplace. At most, research opens up possibilities for marketable products, which then require extended development—a process which can be as lengthy and costly as the initial research. One key ingredient of most development is "scaling up"—taking the initial discovery from something reproducible one at a time and developing the conditions for the large-scale production necessary for commercial success.

For example, although the discovery of penicillin was a major breakthrough, developing it for mass production presented numerous daunting challenges, nearly as difficult to achieve as the original advancement. First discovered in 1928, it was initially raised in laboratory cultures. Of course, only small quantities were required for the clinical research that proved its value, but the processes used to produce these quantities could not be readily adapted for large-scale production. Since the experimental quantities were produced in flasks, the first problem was how to clean hundreds of flasks so no residue remained that would contaminate future batches. The next question to arise was that of producing huge quantities, dispensing it to the flasks, and then autoclaving the flasks so they all received the same heat treatment. This leads to the question of how to measure the inoculums so that each flask received the same amount and then prepare and dispense the spores under antiseptic conditions. Once they were inoculated, each flask would have to be incubated to 24° C. Finally, there was the problem of how to conduct the whole production process so that micro-organisms which might destroy the penicillin would not grow.

Ultimately, large quantities were produced in huge fermentation vats, a process requiring the solution of numerous technical problems. It is particularly interesting that the methods adopted to achieve the production of large quantities created a host of problems as by-products. For instance, the growth medium used was corn steep liquor that had to be aerated so the penicillin would have enough oxygen to grow. But the aeration process—basically, huge mixing paddles turning in enormous vats of the steep liquor—caused the brew to foam, requiring the development of an anti-foaming agent to counteract the side effects of aeration. But the end-result of development efforts was the production of 650 billion units by the end of World War II, with a reduction of cost from $20 per dose in 1942 to 55 cents in 1945.

Technologies which rely on other, complementary technologies to become useful—technologies that are only functional as parts of systems—become ready for diffusion only when complementary technologies on which they depend reach a sufficiently advanced state of development. So, even though the pneumatic tire had been invented twenty years earlier, when bicycles became popular, the invention had been lost and John Dunlop had to re-invent it in 1887. Perhaps one of the most engaging stories of technological development is the tale of how all the components of the electrical system—generators, wiring from power plants to homes, appliances—were developed nearly simultaneously, since no single component had any use unless all the others were fully operational.

Scientific Revolutions

According to Thomas Kuhn, author of *The Structure of Scientific Revolutions*, science advances through periods of cumulative, incremental development (so-called "normal science") punctuated by periods of non-cumulative transformation called "scientific revolutions." During periods of normal science, work progresses under a "paradigm," understood as the conceptual and theoretical framework through which scientists organize experience. Metaphorically, it is sometimes said that paradigms are the lenses through which scientists "see" the world. Paradigms determine:

- the theories accepted and believed by the scientists in the discipline,
- the standards of the field, including the prevailing methodology for experimentation,
- the outstanding puzzles which the paradigm should solve.

Paradigms can only be understood by characterizing their function in the stages preceding, and following upon, the occurrence of a scientific revolution.

During periods of what Kuhn calls "normal science," the paradigm guides the directions in which research is pursued. That is to say, the paradigm identifies the phenomena which its conceptual and theoretical resources might explain. If successful in the explanation of some phenomenon, the paradigm receives further elaboration and articulation by application to a concrete case. In this way, the paradigm redeems the promissory notes issued when it was first accepted. There were, of course, a number of different kinds of reasons for accepting the paradigm at the time of its adoption. One important consideration was the range of new phenomena the paradigm could be used to explain, which earlier paradigms could not. In fact, normal science could be characterized as a period of puzzle-solving as the prevailing paradigm is applied to new phenomena, expanding the scope of phenomena included within the scope of the science. By successfully explaining new phenomena, the paradigm is further confirmed.

Occasionally, researchers will be frustrated in the attempt to apply the paradigm to phenomena which, by all rights, the paradigm should be able to explain. When the efforts to apply the paradigm to a given domain of phenomena are repeatedly frustrated, the domain becomes an anomaly for the paradigm.

Then the scientific community may recognize that the anomaly is a genuine threat to the paradigm and begins the search for a replacement. Or the scientists in the discipline may decide to shelve the explanation of the anomalous phenomena for further work in the future. This may be based on the hope that new techniques and methods will be developed in the future, which will allow the resolution of the anomaly. Typically, the latter course is the one pursued when the prevailing paradigm has been highly successful at explaining phenomena and there is no obvious alternative. In the case of classical mechanics, astronomers become aware as early as the 1820's that the orbit of Mercury deviated from predictions and exhibited unexpected erratic behavior, an advance in its perihelion. But rather than question the Newtonian paradigm, which had proven successful in so many different domains, astronomers simply treated the perihelion of Mercury as a problem to be resolved at some later date, and turned their attention to applying the paradigm to other phenomena. In fact, the perihelion was not explained until Einstein introduced the General Theory of Relativity nearly a century later.

Eventually, unresolved anomalies cause scientists to lose confidence in the prevailing paradigm. At some point, this loss of confidence will led them to begin searching for alternative paradigms which can explain the anomalous phenomena. Once a viable alternative is proposed, the discipline enters a period of crisis, in which the prevailing paradigm is challenged by an alternative, and the individual practitioners begin to investigate the relative merits of the alternatives. This is the beginning of a scientific revolution.

Scientific revolutions are "paradigm-shifts," the abandonment of one paradigm and the acceptance of an alternative in place of the original. Typically, this replacement is a protracted process, beginning with the emergence of anomalies. which undermines the credibility and authority, of the prevailing paradigm. A case like this would be unlike the advance of the perihelion of Mercury, which was simply regarded as an outstanding puzzle which would eventually be resolved. However, when a sufficient number of anomalies have emerged, the scientific community is thrown into a crisis. It would be inaccurate to think that, once the advance of the perihelion of Mercury had been observed, the Newtonian paradigm was in crisis. Indeed, Mercury's anomalous orbit seems to have been quietly relegated to the status of a curiosity, until other, more striking anomalies created a crisis at the turn of the 20th Century.

During a crisis, alternatives to the threatened paradigm are proposed and discussed, and alliances are formed within the community, consisting of groups of practitioners supporting the various alternatives. The most important attribute of the alternatives, according to Kuhn's account, is that they are incommensurable: they are alternative ways of "seeing the world" that simply cannot be compared. In particular, the new proposals are by no means comparable with the threatened paradigm. Some thinkers have argued that the incommensurability of paradigms is a natural consequence of the fact that they employ key terms—like 'mass' in Newtonian and relativistic physics—represent distinct concepts which are differently defined. Another way of making this point is to insist that only those alternative accounts of phenomena that employ genuinely different concepts to organize experience present a competitive alternative to the established paradigm.

The crisis ends, and the revolution is completed, only when one of the proposed alternatives is accepted by a majority of the scientists in the field. This can occur through a dramatic test, in which the proposed paradigm is successful and, ideally, this is what one would expect if the process were fully rational. But in actual scientific practice, what happens frequently falls short of the ideal. All that is required is that a sufficient majority of the scientists in the discipline come to accept one or another of the alternatives. Support may come from any number of directions. Scientists will ally with supporters of a paradigm to improve their position in the field, to draw more attention to their own work, to improve their chances to obtain funding for their research, or to maintain friendships. They need not be swayed by rational considerations like the outcome of experiments, the coherence of the paradigm with other bodies of theory, and so forth. Indeed, such rational grounds for decision-making are often simply unavailable. This is, in part, a consequence of the incommensurability of paradigms. Then the only means available to assist scientists in their choice are not the rational ones mentioned earlier, but the non-rational factors which sway the decision-making process. Indeed, their support may depend entirely on non-rational (but not irrational) factors.

The idea that paradigm shifts are not rational developments is, for many thinkers, rather difficult to accept. It is important to keep in mind, though, that "non-rational" does not mean "irrational." In the context of theory-acceptance, a rational motivation is one which is logically linked to the truth of the theory under

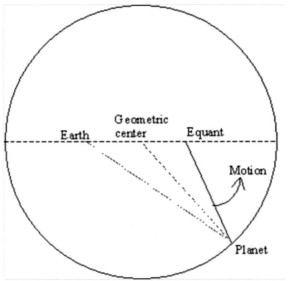

Planetary Orbits in Ptolemaic Astronomy

consideration. So, to say that a motivation for accepting a theory is non-rational is just to say it is based on concerns unrelated to the truth of the theory. It may still be a perfectly good motivation. For instance, one might decide to accept a theory simply because it has been accepted by a particular leader in the field, one who is especially respected and admired for his contributions. Or, one might wish to be identified as one of the supporters of a path-breaking paradigm because the new paradigm raises numerous questions of theoretical interest, which hold great promise of receiving funding in the future, thus improving one's own chances of receiving grants.

What is most important about paradigm-shifts in science is that they represent non-cumulative episodes of scientific development, punctuating the incremental, cumulative development of normal science. These insights, especially the idea that paradigm-shifts result in radically new ways of conceiving experience, have proven fruitful in many other fields. Yet there has been little discussion of whether they might yield exciting new insights if used to supplement the idea accepted by historians, that technological development is always incremental and cumulative. This worn-out cliché seems incapable of explaining innovations that revolutionize technology, and one can only wonder how profoundly our understanding might be altered if revolutions in technology were to be considered in the light of Kuhn's analysis.

Copernicus' Innovation

One of the most contentious elements of Kuhn's analysis of scientific revolutions concerns the incommensurability of competing paradigms. This feature of the crisis stage of revolutions is critical to Kuhn's view because it implies that the adjudication of the competition between an entrenched paradigm and a challenger may not be possible to settle on strictly rational grounds. This consequence introduces a non-rational element into the scientific process, challenging the conventional belief that science is through-and-through rational. These are difficult questions, which cannot be answered in a straightforward manner. Before addressing them, it would be helpful to have a clear-cut example of two genuinely incommensurable competing paradigms. Although the range of possible examples is quite broad, most of them require specialized information to be fully understood. But one of the innovations introduced by Copernicus in his heliocentric planetary scheme marks a dramatic departure from the prevailing paradigm which turns on a shift in the meaning of a key concept.

In earlier discussions of historical astronomy, some of the artificial devices developed so theory would match observation were introduced, like epicycles. Epicycles, it will be recalled, were orbits on orbits, introduced to account for the retrograde motions of planets or to rectify minor discrepancies between prediction and theory. Another device, common in pre-Copernican astronomy, was the equant. Equant points were the centers of the planetary orbits, which were offsets from the earth's position (which was approximately the center of the planetary scheme). The purpose they served was to regularize the comings and goings of the planets to an earthbound observer. For instance, suppose the time which elapses between the appearance of a given planet on the eastern horizon to its disappearance on the western horizon is four months. But the time from its disappearance on the western horizon to its re-appearance on the eastern horizon is five months. It would seem, on the face of matters, that the planet is speeding up and slowing down. But this appearance can be dispelled if it is supposed that the center of the planet's orbit is not exactly the position of the earth, but a point offset from the earth. Then the center of the planet would be this "equant point" and its orbit would be constant and regular, when calculated from the equant point, even though, from an earthbound perspective, the planet seems to speed up and slow down as it goes around the earth.

Since the Middle Ages, astronomers had been suspicious of the equant because it violated the principle that the planets moved in uniform circular motion. Copernicus concurred. He even thought that the equant was fraudulent, because it masked a fundamental inadequacy in any system employing such a device. After all, any account of planetary motion which says, on the one hand, that the planets and the sun orbit around the earth, and then says that the time of their orbits must be calculated from another point, offset from the position of the earth, is duplicitous in the extreme. As Copernicus and all other astronomers up to his time believed, planetary orbits were constant and any scheme that needs an artificial device like the equant to veil an irregularity in planetary motion is a swindle. And subsequent astronomers who read Copernicus' *De Revolutionibus...* agreed that the elimination of the equant was the work's greatest achievement.

Scholars agree that eliminating the equant is one of the major motivations for Copernicus' revolutionary work. Indeed, he thought that the complexity of astronomical systems was justified only on the grounds that it preserved the uniformity of the circular motion of the planets. Not only the orbits of the planets but the planets themselves were considered perfect geometric figures and bodies, since their perimeters were equidistant from their centers. Naturally, perfect bodies traversing perfect orbits must move regularly, uniformly, and constantly. And Copernicus thought that his elimination of the equant restored the meaning of 'constant' when applied to planetary motion. Of course, there were other innovations in Copernicus' scheme, but this was the principal one that made his system truly remarkable.

Notice how this shift in the meaning of "constant" makes Copernicus' heliocentric astronomy incommensurable with Ptolemy's geocentric system. Both a Copernican and a Ptolemaic astronomer would agree that the planetary orbits are made up of constant, circular motion. But the Ptolemaic astronomer allows that the constancy may not be directly observable, from the vantage point of the earth, because the planet may be orbiting an equant point. The Copernican, on the other hand, thinks constancy preserved with equants is not constancy at all but a mask for irregularity. The two are at odds over what they each mean by 'constant' and are, in this respect, incommensurable.

Nor is the case of Copernicus' innovation the only instance in which a new paradigm which challenged an entrenched one was articulated in terms and concepts different in meaning from any in the original theory. Some cases seem to offer little, if any, changes of meaning to create a gulf of incommensurability between competing paradigms. In the case of Priestley's and Lavoisier's chemistries, discussed in Chapter 2, it might be arguable that there simply was no incommensurability. It might be argued that, after all, Lavoisier's "oxygen" just is Priestley's "dephlogisticated air." Thus it might seem as if the inter-translatibility of the key terms of the paradigms dissolves the appearance of incommensurability. Kuhn's thesis of the incommensurability of competing paradigms would seem to fail in such cases. On the other hand, it could well be pointed out that the critical difference between the two chemistry paradigms is only revealed when the relations of the key terms to the other concepts of each of the paradigms. Then it might turn out that, indeed, "oxygen" and "dephlogisticated air" are hardly synonymous, for they bear numerous inferential relations to the other terms of their respective paradigms which vitiates the supposed synonymy. In short, even in cases where there are seemingly interchangeable terms in two competing paradigms, there may yet be considerations that sustain the incommensurability.

The final conclusion that some thinkers have drawn from the

incommensurability of paradigms is there can be no rational, scientific grounds for deciding between competing paradigms. Yet this is clearly incorrect. Certainly, if it were possible to conduct a crucial experiment, as discussed in Chapter 4, between the competing paradigms, then there would indeed be rational grounds for deciding between them. In the case of the Ptolemaic and Copernican paradigms, despite their incommensurability, Galileo conducted observations of the phases of Venus which served as a crucial test of the geocentric and heliocentric paradigms. Obviously, the incommensurability of the astronomical hypotheses did not stop Galileo from finding sound criteria for deciding between them. And what this case shows is simply that the incommensurability does not exclude the possibility of rational adjudication of competing paradigms.

Revolutions in Technology

Certainly, technological development undergoes similar revolutionary phases, in which change and growth in a particular field seems to accelerate overnight. An episode of this sort is the printing revolution of the mid-15th Century.

Before the appearance of the printing press, books were reproduced by scribes, who lovingly but laboriously copied by hand. Even if it assumed that there

Gutenberg and His Printing Press

was a sizable population of scribes, the output would still have been relatively insignificant. But in the first half-century after the invention of the printing press, some eight million books were produced. This was, by any measure, a virtual explosion of texts unlike anything the world had ever seen. Indeed, the invention of the printing press was the most revolutionary development in media technology in history, though it may one day be surpassed by the printing press.

Medieval Paper Mill (from George Agricola's De Re Metallica)

But before this radical development is attributed entirely to the invention of the printing press, a careful examination reveals that it was the result of a number of independent developments, each significant in its own right. First of all, paper had to be developed to replace parchment, which was expensive and time-consuming to produce, since it was the result of laboriously scraping animal skins. Paper had been invented by the Chinese in the Second Century A.D., and disseminated through the Islamic world to the West in the Middle Ages. In Europe, by the end of the 13th Century, paper was produced in water mills for the first time in its 1,000 year history. But the mechanization of paper production depended a specific invention in water mill technology, since making paper depended on pounding rag and other materials. The pounding require the conversion of the rotary motion of the water wheel's shaft into the reciprocating motion of hammers for pounding. This was accomplished by a cam, a lobe on the shaft which caused a bar leaning against the shaft to rise as the lobe first contacted it and fall as the lobe passed by. Paper, mechanically produced, was inexpensive and available in the quantities required for mass production of the books created by the printing press.

Nor was the actual printing press the result of a single insight. To invent the press, Gutenberg had to glimpse two different novel ideas and then envision them combined in a single device. The major challenge lay in the production of the individual blocks of type. Although scholars are uncertain of Johann Gutenberg's original method, it has been established that early print blocks were cast in hand molds. The type Gutenberg created were highly regular and very durable, as evidenced in the inexpensive Bible he printed in the 1450's. Legend has it that Gutenberg's investor, John Fust, took a dozen Bibles to the leading university town, Paris, where they sold so quickly he was run out of town by the guild of the booktrade.

The printing press had dramatic effect on European society in the centuries following its invention because it reached into every corner of culture. It played a key role in the disruption of religious life when Martin Luther mobilized the printing press in behalf of his "reform" movement, letting loose a "roar like a lion across the length and breadth of Europe." In science, scholars across the continent began publishing their discoveries and speculations, as well as reading each other's works. Soon they became a community, exchanging ideas, suggestions, and criticisms. Then an interested scholar isolated in the far northern regions of Prussia, named Nicolaus Copernicus, proposed a radical new understanding of the motion and arrangement of the planets, and the Scientific Revolution was underway. But the printing press affected everyday life in more mundane ways as well. For one thing, governments took advantage of the press to publish edicts, decrees, and new laws. In addition, books on etiquette, child-rearing, and similar topics soon appeared. There were very few facets of daily life which the printing press did not affect.

References

1.   Robert L. Heilbroner, "Do Machines Make History?" in Merritt Roe Smith and Leo Marx, ed. *Does Technology Drive History?* (Cammbridge, MA: MIT Press, 1994). pp. 56-7.

2.   W. G. L. de Haas, "Technology as a Subject of Comparative Studies: The Case of Photography," *Comparative Studies in Society and History*, Vol. 21, No. 3 (Jul., 1979), P. 369.

3.   Jacob Schmookler. *Inventions and Economic Growth.* (Cambridge, MA: Harvard University Press, 1966).

4.   David Perlman, "The History of Penicillin Production," in Albert Elder, ed. *The History of the Production of Penicillin.* (New York: American Institute of Chemical Engineers, 1970). P. 25.

5.   Thomas Kuhn. *The Copernican Revolution.* (Cambridge: Harvard University Press, 1957). P. 71.

6.   Owen Gingerich. *The Book Nobody Read.* (New York: Walker and Company, 2004). Pp. 23n, 53.

7.   Gingerich, p. 55.

8.   Kuhn. Pp. 70-1.

9.   Nicolaus Copernicus. "Commentariolus," Edward Rosen, trans. In Edward Rosen, ed. *Three Copernican Treatises.* (Mineola, NY: Dover Publications, 1939). P. 57.

10.   Michael Clapham, "Printing," in Charles Singer, E. G. Holmyard, A. R. Hall, and Trevor Williams, eds. *A History of Technology.* Vol. 3. From the Renaissance to the Industrial

Revolution. (Oxford: Oxford University Press, 1957), P. 57.

11. Burns, Robert I. (1996). "Paper comes to the West, 800–1400". In Lindgren, Uta. Europäische Technik im Mittelalter. 800 bis 1400. Tradition und Innovation (4th ed.). Berlin: Gebr. Mann Verlag. pp. 413–422.

12. Jean Gimpel. *The Medieval Machine: The Industrial Revolution of the Middle Ages.* (New York: Penguin Books, 1976). P. 14.

13. S. Ozment. *The Age of Reform*, 1250-1550. (New Haven: Yale University Press, 1980). P. 33.

EXERCISES

Multiple-Choice

_____ 1. An important difference between science and technology is the dynamic of their _____.
Technology progresses _____, accumulating changes to preceding innovations.
   a. development ... incrementally
   b. proliferation ... worldwide
   c. market ... profitably
   d. funding ... instantly

_____ 2. Successful innovation depends largely on the innovators' perceptions of _____.
   a. political pressure.
   b. consumer wants and needs.
   c. popular opinion.
   d. global climate.

_____ 3. Key to the successful acceptance of an innovation is whether effective demand exists in society—that is, the _____ for the product and the ability to _____ for it.
   a. idea ... visualize
   b. hope ... dream
   c. design ... adjust
   d. desire ... pay

_____ 4. The product development stage of technology transforms a _____ innovation into a _____ invention.
   a. creative ... compelling
   b. functional ... miraculous
   c. workable ... competitively priced
   d. mundane ... irresistible

5. Great successes in the improvement of a technology seldom result from _____; more often than not, they are the result of a _____ about what might work.
   a. flashes of brilliance; ... a clever hunch
   b. deliberate testing; ... sudden epiphany
   c. cooperative effort; ... single idea
   d. lone innovators; ... collective opinion

True/False

1. Science operates under the demands of its sponsors who supervise the scientists working for them quite closely.
2. When the camera first appeared in the early 19th Century, it provided an affordable means for the lower classes to imitate more affluent members of society.
3. Consumers are the best predictors of their own wants and needs.
4. Basic research is time consuming, expensive, and seldom results in market-ready products.
5. The mass production of penicillin was a long and arduous process requiring many small innovations to scale up production in sufficient quantities at a low enough cost.
6. A scientific occurs when enough anomalies have been encountered in the standing theory's ability to explain observed phenomena to require new theoretical foundations.
7. New paradigms supplant their predecessors only when they have been proven by rigorous tests.
8. The Enlightenment engendered a general distrust of science out of a preference for the human spirit.
9. Technology develops cumulatively.

_____ 10. The incommensurability of paradigms is a natural consequence of the fact that some of the key concepts of competing paradigms are differently understood.

Discussion Questions

1.   By this point, you know enough to identify paradigms shifts that have occurred in scientific thought. Think of one or two paradigms shifts. Who did these paradigm shifts affect (scientists, engineers, scholars, average people)? How did the shifts change the worldview and the day-to-day actions of the groups you have identified?

2.   Technology develops incrementally. In fact, many companies now take advantage of incremental development by creating new "generations" of devices. Do you think it's ethical for companies to promote the replacing of older models—that are still working—for the newer generation? What are the positive effects of this type of production and consumption? What are the negative effects?

3.   Paradigm-shifts occur in daily life all the time, sometimes called "Aha!" or "Eureka!" moments. Describe one from your own life, identify the initial paradigm, its competition, and what led you to shift.

6

THE SOCIAL CONTEXT

> One class presses on another; for
> all are aiming to procure respect on
> account of their property: and property,
> once gained, will procure the respect
> due only to talents and virtue....
>
> -Mary Wollstonecraft,
> *A Vindication of the Rights of Woman*

Society is a collection of individuals who have come together for a purpose. More often, they associate with one another for a host of purposes, which may be the same, or not, depending on the individual or the circumstances. The reasons people gather in groups and associate range from mutual defense, sociability, to simply improving their access to whatever satisfies their wants and needs. There are obvious costs and benefits of mutual association, and when people come together in groups voluntarily, it is because they have judged that the potential benefits outweigh the foreseeable costs.

Social Groups

Once brought together in a social group, individuals form sub-groups based on more closely allied interests, like common origins, shared hobbies, and so forth. For instance, within associations of ethnically similar individuals, say Americans of

Italian origin, all the writers and poets may join together, thus forming a sub-group of Italian-American writers and poets. The members of the group may also form sub-groups to pursue certain social objectives, to encourage the society as a whole to pursue certain goals which particularly benefit their sub-group. Examples of groups advocating social changes beneficial for their members might be the Society of Retired Locomotive Engineers or the American Association of Retired Persons. Other sub-groups, who perceive that the costs will outweigh the benefits for their sub-group, may discourage society's pursuit of the same goal. For that matter, it seems that every time a group forms to promote social change, other groups form to oppose and prevent the change, like Pro-Choice and Pro-Life groups. Thus society consists of sub-groups competing for the goods that their mutual association in the larger social body has to offer.

The interests which bring individuals into groups have been thoroughly studied by folklorists. And folklorists have discovered a cornucopia of pretexts for the formation of groups. Individuals might gather together because they share an interest in model trains, Harley-Davidson motorcycles, or the escapades of the Royal Family. Group membership might also be conditioned on the basis of similar dress, common habits, or passage through common initiation rites. What binds individuals into groups is infinitely varying and endlessly intriguing.

It is, of course, widely recognized that the effects of scientific and technological developments affect society in multifarious ways. And these may range from the dramatic to the trivial. But understanding the function of science and technology in society also requires drawing out the effects that social structure has on science and technology. The fact that society is partitioned into subgroups, each seeking their own advantage, and that the partitioning shifts and changes relative to different questions and purposes, implies that there will be a fluctuation of groups supporting particular research directions in science or certain avenues of technological development. The same group that opposes stem cell research might split into two groups divided over the funding of, say, diabetes research. How this continual alignment and re-alignment of interests affects the advancement of science or the development of technology is an exciting topic. It is also a topic riddled with faulty thinking, consisting mostly of hasty generalizations. What results sound great on a bumper sticker or a political slogan, but fold under the scrutiny of careful analysis.

Of course, occupational interests are another group-defining

ACCADEMIA DEI LINCEI

characteristic, so it would be no surprise to learn that the creators of science and technology form professional associations, working groups, and other associations. It should be noted, from the outset, that scientific research and technological development are social enterprises. Both depend on the cooperation of countless professionals, interacting in pursuit of a common goal. The image of the lone scientist working late at night in his lab to make the discovery of a lifetime is simply not an accurate depiction of scientists today. This picture may once have reflected scientific practice, but even before the Scientific Revolution, scientific advance has increasingly depended on the exchanges of individual scientists. Indeed, the invention of the printing press in 1453 contributed significantly to the communication among scientists and, in an important sense, made possible the innovations of Copernicus, Galileo, Kepler, and Newton. In fact, it was shortly after the publication of Galileo's Siderius Nuncius in 1610 that Kepler corresponded with him, congratulating him on his confirmations of Copernican heliocentrism and sharing his own speculations about the origins of the craters on the moon. The tendency to increase the community of specialists involved in science became a hallmark of the Scientific Revolution, leading to the creation of scientific societies like the *Accedemia dei Lincei* in 1603 and the Royal Society of London in 1660. This tendency has continued ever since.

Of course, scientists and engineers belong to various professional societies, organized by professions, by specialties, by research interests, and myriad other ways. Perhaps more dramatic proof can be drawn from the collective research published in journals. For instance, in 1963, sixty-four names were cited as authors of the article "First Measurement of the Left-Right Cross Section Asymmetry in Z-Boson Production by e + e Collisions," published in *Physical Review Letters. The same is true of engineers, but even more obvious proof* is provided by the research facilities of major corporations, in which vast numbers of engineers work together to produce the breakthroughs that keep the corporations profitable. Even Thomas Edison realized that his revolutionary insights could never become functional devices without the assistance of a troop of well-qualified assistants. It has been said that the industrial research laboratory Edison ran in Menlo Park, New Jersey was the first of its kind. And it might well be said that Edison's greatest achievement was to invent the business of invention itself.

Social Consequences

At one extreme lie those developments that totally

disrupt the existing social order. For instance, the Yir Yoront, an Australian stone-age tribe, structured their power and religious relationships around stone hand axes. The axes symbolized many of the aspirations and expectations of the males of the tribe, for whom they were prized possessions. Only males could possess axes, even though many of the tasks requiring an axe were performed by women. Obviously, this social arrangement sustained the value of male supremacy among the tribe. Indeed, adolescent males planned how they would make their own axes, well in advance of maturity, when they would actually begin to make them. These plans included how the axes would be fashioned from the available materials, how the necessary materials would be acquired, and so on. In fact, obtaining the stones for the axe heads involved a complex network of trading relations, for the stones came from as far as 200 miles away. When missionaries visited, they rewarded the labors of all tribe members—regardless of age or gender—who assisted them with steel axes, which were highly prized by the Yir Yoront. Soon, the entire social order, based on the stone axes, disintegrated.

At the other extreme, lie instances in which technology is introduced solely for the purpose of preserving the status quo. Perhaps the best-known case occurred in the McCormick reaper factory, at a time when skilled workers—members of a powerful union—fashioned the fenders of the reapers by hand. To break the power of the union, thus preventing any efforts to seek higher wages, management introduced pneumatic molding machines, which created the fenders from molds and replaced the workers. In fact, the new machines produced an inferior fender, at greater cost to the company. After several years, the "fender benders" were re-hired to mold the fenders, at the wages paid to unskilled workers. And the pneumatic molding machines? They were scrapped.

Sometimes groups will resist the introduction of new technologies to protect their position in society. For instance, a home manufacturer introduced "service cores" consisting of the kitchen, bathroom, and utility room (as well as all necessary wiring and plumbing) as factory-built units after World War II, but union workers refused to install them without first completely disassembling and rebuilding them, which made them prohibitively expensive. In another case, British manufacturers built a factory to increase productivity of silk, traditionally a cottage industry in China. The British venture failed because members of the silk-makers' guild, who traditionally controlled the monopoly in silk production, forced cocoon producers to raise prices, leading to an increased price of their basic raw material—silkworm cocoons.

The salient conclusion that follows from these examples is that [scientific and technological developments always affect the structure of the social group into which they are introduced]. The lesson to be learned from these examples is that the consequences of the implementation of a technology may sometimes seem to advance, frustrate, or even diminish the position of a social group in society. And social groups will always attempt to use scientific advances and technological developments to protect and improve their position in society.

Even when the introduction of a new technology appears to have only beneficial consequences, there are always detrimental effects. In the 1960's, railroad cars were developed that could carry a large number of automobiles from the factories to central terminals, and from there the autos could be easily distributed to dealerships by truck. This arrangement had obvious benefits: delivery costs would be reduced, thus increasing dealer profits as well as consumer savings. But the over-the-road truck drivers, who had been delivering cars to the dealers all the way from the factories for many years, were denied an important source of income, prompting them to protest publicly and—in some extreme cases—commit acts of vandalism. Although social groups that are disadvantaged by technological change may not resort to radical measure to prevent or reverse developments affecting them adversely, it is only natural to expect them to respond.

Luddism=anyone who is opposed to technology in general

Like Ned Ludlum and his co-workers, who rioted when the stocking-frame was introduced to replace workers in British textile mills in the early 19th Century, the truckers were not objecting to technological innovation in general, or even to the new railcars in particular. Rather, the new technologies—whether the stocking-frame or auto-carrier—symbolized a weakening of their financial position, a reduction of their power as a social group. In Ludlum's day, the British textile workers were, after all, subjected to repeated tax increases, as well as increases in the costs of foodstuffs, as a result of the Napoleonic wars. The introduction of the stocking-frames—which actually produced shoddier stockings with little cost reduction—was the proverbial "straw that broke the camel's back," pushing the workers beyond the point at which they could control their responses. So they attacked the factory buildings—including the manager's home—and burned several of the buildings.

Of course, the term "Luddite" has evolved considerably in the last two hundred years, and as commonly understood today, signifies anyone who is opposed to technology in general. Such an attitude is hardly admirable, since it uncritically lumps together useful technologies, which benefit millions like the Salk vaccine for polio, with those which have few, if any, positive benefits.

An equally uncritical attitude is exemplified by those who regard every technological innovation, regardless of scale, importance to the broad masses of humanity, or contribution to the human condition, as a monumental advance. But although there have been few true Luddites who unilaterally rejected all technological innovation, there have been many notable champions of technology.

Indeed, many influential leaders of American society in the 19th Century celebrated the products of the Industrial Revolution as the zenith of humanity's aspirations. It is particularly important to keep in mind that the products they celebrated were simply mass-produced geegaws and trinkets, hardly innovations that advanced civilization.

Walt Whitman

Still, Ralph Waldo Emerson exclaimed that "the golden age is before, not behind us." And Mark Twain, who was always enamored of technical gadgets, proclaimed his century to be "the plainest and sturdiest and infinitely greatest and worthiest of all the centuries the world has seen." He even congratulated the poet Walt Whitman for having been fortunate to live in the age that gave the world coal tar (which was used to fuel lanterns)! It is worth mentioning that one need only read Henry David Thoreau to realize that these attitudes were not universally shared. For that matter, *The Adventures of Huckleberry Finn* is Twain's own celebration of lifestyles and values untouched by the technological advances of the Industrial Revolution.

Technological Fixes

It would seem plausible to think that social problems, or at least some of them, might be remedied by developing and introducing the right technology. Unfortunately, experience shows that this is just the first of a whole series of misconceptions about how technology and society interact. If, indeed, a problem has its roots in some social arrangement, then it is doubtful that any "technological fix" can possibly remedy it, despite the repeated efforts of optimists. And the problem with a technological fix should be readily apparent: after all, a technological fix is (by definition!) an attempt to provide a technical solution to a social problem. In the first place, technical solutions only succeed when the difficulty is itself technical in nature. And by that nothing more is meant than that the system in which the problem occurs is limited to purely technical causes and effects. For instance, when the steering wheel of a car vibrates between 65 and 70 miles per hour, it is safe to say that the cause is purely mechanical. It is totally unrelated to the phases of the moon, the conjunction of Jupiter and Saturn, the driver's karma, or even her guilty conscience. Thus, the problem is a completely mechanical (and thus technical) problem, and it may be safely inferred that a technical solution will succeed.

But social problems are of a mixed variety, with very few technical components. Recall that the Luddite riots of the early 1800's were not caused just by the introduction of stocking-frames. Certainly, the new technology played a role in triggering the violent reaction of the workers, but the complete story is a more complicated affair. And this is typical of social problems and solutions in which science and technology play a role. At most, science and technology figure as partial causes, incapable of bringing about the effect in question on their own. Rather, it is only in conjunction with other factors, typically neither scientific nor technological, that a technical innovation can bring about the specific effect. Consequently, no technological fix can possibly remedy the situation, at least not on its own.

A good example of this kind of multi-modal causation can be found in the origins of the Protestant Reformation, described in the previous chapter. It will be recalled that the

Reformation was triggered when Martin Luther posted his 95 theses on the door of the Wittenberg Castle Church in 1517. If the matter had ended there, that the theses were never printed and distributed throughout the duchies, principalities, and kingdoms of (what would eventually become) Germany, then it may be safely supposed that Luther would have been tried as a heretic, found guilty, punished, and that would have been the end of the matter. This supposition, though purely speculative, is nonetheless highly plausible, given what is known about other attempts to reform the Church during the period. And, of course, it is well-known that the contribution of the printing press, invented by Johannes Gutenberg in Mainz in 1453, was indispensable to the publication of Luther's theses, their distribution throughout the northern provinces of Germany, and the subsequent popularization of Luther's complaints. Indeed, within two years, Luther's theses had reached England, France, and Italy. As one scholar remarked, "The Protestant Reformation was the first religious movement to have the aid of the printing press."

⁑ By the same token, it is equally true that, without Luther, the printing press would never have brought about the Protestant Reformation, as it actually occurred. Thus, Luther's action was just as necessary a cause of the Reformation as the invention of the printing press: each acted as a partial cause, without which the effect would never have occurred.

Indeed, there are a whole class of problems which simply do not admit of a scientific or technological solution. Consider the theoretical problem known as "the Tragedy of the Commons." Prior to the passage of the land enclosure laws in 17th Century England, small leaseholders accessed an open area, called "the commons," which was shared among the other small leaseholders of the village. (To this day, the open area in front of the Massachusetts State House is called "The Boston Commons.") Typically, the commons were used for grazing sheep, which would increase the food supplies of the participating villagers.

Each villager, in pursuit of his own self-interest, should naturally attempt to graze as many sheep as he possibly can, thus maximizing his benefit. Of course, the dilemma which then arises is that, if every villager pursues the same strategy, they will succeed only as long as the commons does not

Grazing on the Commons

become over-grazed. Then, of course, no one will benefit. Problems of this sort admit no technical—that is, scientific or technological solution—but require, in the words of the noted ecologist Garrett Hardin, a fundamental extension in morality. These problems typically involve social arrangements utilizing limited natural resources.

Throughout history, people have repeatedly ignored the failures of technological fixes and continued to place their trust in technology. This tendency reached its height when an engineer, Herbert Hoover, was elected president in 1928. Hoover's popularity rested, to a large extent, on his success directing relief efforts after the Mississippi flood of 1927, which displaced literally hundreds of thousands along the mighty river, from the vicinity of Missouri and Illinois all the way downriver to New Orleans. Actually, Hoover hired professional press officers to present his efforts to the public. They created the impression of a smooth, well-coordinated effort that was largely successful. More recent research, however, reveals that the rescue efforts were a disaster on top of the original disaster;

its successes attributable to others as much to Hoover, and its darker sides carefully suppressed by Hoover's press agents at his direction. For instance, more than 13,000 African American sharecroppers were marooned on a levee near Greenville, Mississippi, and forced to work on the barricades at gunpoint, with no food or clean water for several days. Eventually, the tension erupted and a wave of violence directed at the blacks broke out in the hardest hit areas of Mississippi and Arkansas. In a few cases, the violence even resulted in lynchings. It would, of course, be wrong to charge Hoover with responsibility for the treatment of the African Americans, but, at the same time, the flood control and relief efforts were hardly the shining success what was portrayed in the popular press. Still, on the basis of these reports, Hoover was elected president in 1928.

Unsurprisingly, when the Great Depression began in the first year of Hoover's presidency, he found himself at a complete loss to appreciate the nature, extent, and treatment of the economic calamity. One result was that he was memorialized in countless "Hoovervilles" across America, whole towns of cardboard, sheet metal, and scrapwood shacks populated by the homeless and unemployed. Of course, Hoover can hardly be held responsible for the Great Depression, but at the same time, it is undeniable that he did nothing to alleviate the privations of millions of suffering Americans.

The moral of the story, like the lessons to be drawn from any failed attempt to remedy social ills with technology, is simply that technological fixes work best on technical systems. The chances of successfully remedying a social problem with a technological fix is inherently limited by the fact that such problems, by their very nature, are always caused—at least partially—by social factors.

Technological Determinism

Even though there are always external influences playing into the development of a technology, there are still questions about their relative weight. This is just to wonder whether a given technological idea would be realized as the same or similar concrete artifact if it were developed in different social contexts. Or is technological development driven by its own inner dynamic? This is just the question of whether technological change is primarily the product of internal technical concerns. In other words, is technological development deterministic? Of course, the same kind of determinism is often attributed to scientific advances, as if the pursuit of a program of research and discovery were dictated solely by the subject matter of the study.

Related to this question is a second one concerning the deterministic character of technological change but in a different respect. This question has to do with the effect of technology on society and addresses the similarity of technological effects on different societies. In other words, it raises the question whether a given technology produces the same effect when introduced to different societies.

The idea that technology is deterministic in the first sense, the sense in which technology develops according to its own inner dynamic, springs from reflection on the pre-conditions of the development of any given technology. If one just considers what would be required before a society could even produce a technology like a steam locomotive, one soon realizes that a range of technological achievements are absolutely necessary. For one thing, materials technologies would have to have reached an advanced stage of development, in order to produce the iron and steel required for fabricating the boilers, wheels, and tracks required by a steam locomotive. Certainly it would be difficult to conceive the production of steam locomotives if the 60 years of industrial development had not transpired beforehand. In this time, inventors and engineers struggled through the difficult early stages of development of the stationary steam engine, the technology of metal production, and the organization of steam-powered factories.

Steam Locomotive

But this realization is by no means convincing proof of determinism in technological development. For one thing, the concerns raised are strictly retrospective, looking backwards from a given technological achievement to see what came earlier that was essential. Certainly, it does not substantiate the possibility of prediction of future technologies, by allowing a survey of existing technologies and foretelling what will be developed in the future, at least not with any specificity. This is extremely significant. It will be recalled from the "Introduction" that Simon LaPlace's original characterization of determinism spelled it out in terms of prediction and retrodiction. If a given stage of technological development does not provide an adequate basis for predicting –with a fair amount of specificity- the next stage, the technological development is not deterministic. If knowledge of a given phase of technological advance does not yield knowledge of future stages, then technological determinism is not deterministic in LaPlace's sense.

A second shortcoming of the argument is its failure to recognize the equally important requirement of trained personnel to construct, maintain, and repair new technologies. For instance, the move from the early stage of the Industrial Revolution to the creation of the railroads required trained metalworkers and highly skilled machinists. The early stages of the Industrial Revolution produced workers who possessed the basis of skills needed to build the railroads and keep the trains running.

There are two equal and opposite reactions to this point. On the one hand, it might be argued that these considerations provide persuasive grounds for technological determinism. On the other, it might be argued that the move from a stationary steam engine powering factories to its deployment as a motive force is akin to the emergence of a new variety within an already well-established species.

What determinism misses is the role of the human actors who conceive and develop scientific and technological ideas. And these human actors are social animals, who achieve solutions by working together. This insight sheds light on many errors in the narrative accounts of important advances in science or dramatic developments in technology. Too often these accounts rely on a version of the "great man" approach to history, which attributes responsibility for key events to particular individuals operating in a specific place and time. But these accounts usually only succeed by neglecting the essential function of the great man's close associates, relations with other workers in his field, or simply the social milieu in which he lived. For instance, while there is no denying Thomas Edison's inventive genius, the fact is that his greatest accomplishment is the assembly of bright, young inventors gathered around him at his laboratory at Menlo Park.

The failure of technological determinism to recognize the role of human agents gathered into social groups afflicts not only the way in which new technologies emerge from existing ones, but the social reactions to technological innovation as well. Technological determinists who think that a given technology will evoke the same or a similar response from different social groups simply neglect the way in which these reactions are shaped, influenced, and directed not by the persons and groups they affect. Perhaps the most dramatic story of this type is the account, told by the historian Lynn White, of how the feudal system arose from the introduction of the humble stirrup in medieval France.

Although the earliest stirrups have been found in Asia and dated from the pre-Christian era, they did not appear in

Medieval Stirrup

Europe until the mid-8th Century. Because of the stirrup's effect on the rider's stability and on his competence leveraging the heavy combat weapons of the day, the introduction of the stirrup immediately had a profound effect on combat. Prior to the stirrup's adoption, a mounted warrior was little more than an infantry soldier who was riding rather than walking to the next engagement. Because of the stirrup, the mounted warrior soon became an armored arsenal, bristling with weapons of every size and shape, including daggers, swords, battle-axes, and lances. In White's phrase, Medieval "shock troops." With the leverage provided by the stirrup, the knight could engage his enemy from a mounted position, wielding his weapons with great force while nimbly evading the assaults of his foe. This new type of warfare transformed the clash of armies into a collection of simultaneous battles between individual protagonists. Gone was the order and discipline which characterized the victorious armies of the Roman Empire.

The individualism created by the type of fighting that evolved made its protagonists into small-time entrepreneurs offering their services to the highest bidder. The knight's retinue, including mounts, armor, weapons, and squires was costly and the nobles at the time were land-poor. So they offered the knights grants of land in exchange for the obligation to provide military service, as the need arose. These grants were given in perpetuity, so that the knight and his offspring were forever the vassals of the noble granting them land and his descendants. The knight became a vassal and the noble became the knight's liege lord. The liege-lord would, in turn, be the vassal of another noble, or perhaps a king, who had initially granted him his holdings.

And so the form of social organization known as "feudalism" evolved as a reaction to the stirrup. Of course, this history would substantiate the thesis that technology determines social structure only if a host of contributing factors are ignored. There is, first of all, the pre-existing patterns of social organization prior to the introduction of the stirrup. The nobility was already established, derived from Frankish origins, but their control over the populations of their respective domains was weak and ineffectual. Their resources were extremely limited, and their tax revenues were typically paid in goods and services. So the stirrup came at a time when the social organizations were weak and in dire need of the means to give it greater strength. One other weakness stems from the fact that, when the stirrup was adopted throughout Chinese society, it had no obvious effect on the social structure. And this is just a glimpse of the kinds of flaws which might be revealed by a careful examination of the historical conditions in which the stirrup was introduced. But even this quick peek reveals exactly how weakly the example of the stirrup substantiates the thesis that technology determines the social structure.

Social Constructionism

At the other end of the spectrum, standing in contrast to determinism, is the idea of social construction or, in other words, the notion that the key ingredient in any groundbreaking development is the interaction between interested individuals. "Social Construction" is one of those terms used quite fluidly so that, for instance, some theorists maintain that all technologies are social constructions. It sounds like they are defending the idea that groups of people get together and collectively think an artifact into existence, which is, of course, ridiculous. What they actually mean is: the meaning and significance of an artifact, the use to which it is put and the role it assumes in human interactions, is entirely determined by the social group which creates, produces, and uses it.

Their principal argument is just the simple idea that the significance of a device is entirely determined by it use. Use, in turn, is a function of the social consensus. A clear example of this reasoning is the use of the internet to send email. Originally, the Army created the internet to expedite the sharing of files between and among research facilities, both national defense and universities. Suddenly, without any explicit planning, the internet was being used to send personal messages among workers at the institutions connected by the net. Although one purpose may have driven the original conception and guided its design, the internet took on a wholly distinct significance when put to the unanticipated use of sending personal messages, now known as "email."

technologies = social constructs

Conclusion

The topic of social constructionism returns the discussion to its starting point: the ubiquity of science and technology in the course of everyday life. This inquiry began by remarking on the indisputable fact that scientific advances and technological innovations seemed to force their ways into daily life, invading and conquering every domain of our activities, from work to play to social interaction. Indeed, the very title of this book raises questions about how life is lived in the 21st Century, on a day-by-day, minute-by-minute basis.

There is simply no denying that science and technology permeate everything we do, whether it is eating, sleeping, working, or enjoying ourselves and the company of others. This fact naturally led to the question of how the current situation came about, and a solution was sought by looking into the reasoning processes which, in case by case and decision after decision, brought us to this point. The inevitable conclusion is that the situation in which we find ourselves is the product of our own best choices, made in the pursuit of our dreams.

By increasing our awareness of the consequences of our choices, enhancing our cognizance of the fact that we owe the very texture of our lives to the advances of science and the inventions of technology, we can heighten our awareness of the factors figuring in our calculations, making them just that much wiser than they might otherwise have been.

References

1.   Abe K, et al. "First Measurement of the Left-Right Cross Section Asymmetry in Z-Boson Production by e + e Collisions," *Physical Review Letters* Apr 26, 1993;70 (17), pp. 2515-2520.

2.   Lauriston Sharp, "Steel Axes for Stone Age Australians," Edward H. Spicer, ed. *Human Problems in Technological Change.* Russell Sage Foundation (1952), pp. 69-81.

3.   Langdon Winner, "Do Artifacts Have Politics?" *Daedalus* 109, 1 (Winter 1980), pp. 123-125.

4.   Peter Blake. *Form Follows Fiasco: Why Modern Architecture Hasn't Worked.* (Boston: Little Brown, 1974).

5.   Malcolm I. Thomis. *The Luddites: Machine-Breaking in Regency England.* (New York: Schocken Books, 1972).

6.   Neil Postman. *Building a Bridge to the 18th Century.* (New York: Vintage Books, 1999). Pp. 37-8.

7.   Louise Holborn, "Printing and the Growth of a Protestant Movement in Germany from 1517-1524," *Church History* XI (June 1942), p. 51.

8.   Garrett Hardin, "The Tragedy of the Commons," *Science* 162 (13 December 1968), pp. 1243-1248.

9.   John M. Barry. *Rising Tide.* (New York: Touchstone Books, 1998). Pp. 17-171.

10. Barry, Ch. 27.

11. Christopher   Gray,   "Streetscapes: Central   Park's

'Hooverville'; Life Along 'Depression Street,'" *New York Times* (August 29, 1993).

12. George E. Davidson. *Beehives of Invention: Edison and His Laboratories*. National Park Service History Series. (Washington: Department of the Interior, 1973). http://www.nps.gov/history/online_books/hh/edis/edisc.htm

13. Lynn White, Jr. *Medieval Technology and Social Change*. (Oxford: Oxford University Press, 1962). Pp. 1-38.

14. Bernard S. Bachrach, "Charles Martel, Mounted Shock Combat, the Stirrup, and Feudal Origins," *Studies in Medieval and Renaissance History*. 7 (1970), pp. 47-76.

15. Joseph Needham. *Science and Civilization*, Vol. V, Part 1, p. 365.

EXERCISES

Multiple-Choice

_____ 1. Pneumatic molding machines were installed in the McCormick Reaper Factory to
   a. produce better fenders for their famous reapers.
   b. lower the cost of producing fenders.
   c. create a pre-text for laying off skilled workers.
   d. to make the workers' jobs easier.

_____ 2. Which of the following statements is true.
   a. After World War II, union workers readily installed "service cores" because this invention made their jobs easier.
   b. The implementation of a new technology always affects social groups equally.
   c. Silk makers in China easily accepted the British take-over of the silk industry.
   d. Technology is never completely beneficial; there are always detrimental effects.

_____ 3. Social Constructionists believe that social groups
   a. come together to build things.
   b. think technological artifacts into existence.
   c. determine the meaning and significance of new technologies.
   d. play no role in decisions to extend research funding.

_____ 4. The "great man" approach to technological and scientific history attributes significant developments to _____.
   a. lone individuals working at a particular time.
   b. the person in power at the time of the breakthrough.
   c. eminent figures who actually had nothing to do with the development.
   d. all of the above.

_____ 5. Herbert Hoover's platform of "technocracy" is famous for its faith in the "technological fix," which is
   a. method of giving society new technologies when they want them.
   b. an attempt to apply a technological solution to a social problem.
   c. an attempt to apply a non-technical solution to a mechanical problem.
   d. easy way to solve problems.

True/False

_____ 1. Groups within a society are constant; there is no change or shift of groups supporting a particular research direction in science or certain avenues of technological development.

_____ 2. The innovation of the printing press increased communication among scientists.

_____ 3. Technology can be introduced to reinforce the status quo.

_____ 4. The original Luddites were responding, in part, to the oncrous taxes imposed as a result of the Napoleonic wars.

_____ 5. The thesis of Technological Determinism is just the belief that technology develops according to its own inner dynamic, independently of social forces.

_____ 6. Thomas Edison worked alone in his laboratory in Menlo Park.

_____ 7. Technological determinism is the belief that the significance of a device is entirely determined by its use.

_____ 8. "The Tragedy of the Commons" illustrates a dilemma that cannot be solved by technology but only by morality.

_____ 9. Technological determinism does not account for

the stirrup's influence on both warfare and society in Medieval Europe because other societies that adopted it did not develop feudalism.

_____ 10. Martin Luther would have effectively started a religious revolution even if the printing press hadn't been invented.

Discussion Questions

1.   The internet was intended for use by universities and defense facilities; however, workers at these institutions used the internet to send personal messages, e-mail. What other inventions can you think of that where made for one purpose and used for another? If you were an inventor, would you be disappointed if your invention was used for some purpose other than that for which you intended it? Why or why not?

2.   Have you ever justified a purchase of a new technology by claiming that it would fix a "social" problem? When? What was the technology? What was the problem? Did it work? Discuss what you were hoping would happen and what actually happened.

3.   Hoover was elected because of his platform of "technocracy." Would you vote for someone who proposed to fix social problems with technology? Why or why not? Can you think of any examples of positions on political issues that are based on a technological fix?

4.   As is shown by the example of the British building a silk-producing factory (a factory which would undermine the local silk merchants' livelihood and which was fortunately abandoned in this circumstance), often the introduction of new technology threatens an established business. What are some businesses that our pursuit of cleaner energy will force us to abandon? What are some businesses that our reliance on the Internet will threaten? Can you think of any other examples of this?